Happy Healthy Family
Tracking the Outdoors In

Happy Healthy Family Tracking the Outdoors In

Stacy Harris

GRAY FOREST PUBLISHING LLC
Pike Road, Alabama

Happy Healthy Family Tracking The Outdoors In
Copyright © 2011 By Stacy Harris

First Edition: October 2011

Softcover ISBN: 978-0-9838799-0-9

eBook ISBN: 978-0-9838799-1-6

ePub ISBN: 978-0-9838799-2-3

1. Cooking 2. Wild Game 3. Hunting 4. Meals 5. Entertaining 6. Health foods

I. Harris, Stacy II. Title

Happy Healthy Family Tracking the Outdoors In may be purchased at special quantity discounts to use as corporate premiums, sales promotions, corporate training programs, gifts, fund raising, book clubs, or educational purposes for schools and universities. For more information contact stacypilgreenharris@gmail.com.

To reach people around the globe in their own language, we have a rights and licensing department. For translation or reprint rights in English or any other language in book or electronic format contact Mel Cohen, 1000 Pearl Road Pleasantville, TN 37033, 931-593-2484 or email Mel at melcohen@hughes.net.

www.gameandgarden.com

Publisher:
Gray Forest Publishing LLC
Pike Road, AL 36064

Photography: David Robertson, David Robertson, Jr., Stacy Harris

Cover design and layout: Lynne Hopwood

Printed in China.

Thanks

First I would like to thank my family for encouraging me to write this book and acting as my awesome assistants. It has been so much fun working with you all in the kitchen, setting up for the photography, and taste testing the recipes with you, which I think are everybody's favorites! The organized chaos could not have been more fun than it has been with you.

So many people helped me in the producing of this book. I cannot thank enough, a genius of a man, Mel Cohen, who led me step by step through the publishing and the marketing process and did his best to please me and keep me grounded and informed, and Lynne Hopwood who gave me exactly what I wanted in the design of the book. Thank you so very much for paying attention to the many details!

I also want to thank David Robertson, David Robertson, Jr., and their staff for taking such beautiful photographs of my family, home, and me, and for all your encouragement and advice. It has been priceless. Many thanks to Lana Hayden of Lynn Mathison Interiors for prop design in the family photographs.

Finally, thanks to my mom, Paula Johnson, and friends Paula McWhorter and Sherri Holding who have supported me in this venture, and for Johnny Harris and Rene McCollum for helping me to learn how to use my Canon camera. I appreciate you all so much.

Dedications

For Scott, Hunter, Hampton, Graylyn, Howlett, Mary Elizabeth, Anna Julia, and Milly.

For Scott, without whom I could not have written this cookbook, in that, I would know nothing of wild game without his incredible expertise in harvesting them. You could not make me happier. You have exceeded my expectations of a husband and father. Thank you for being with the children and me every moment you have, apart from your dental practice, and teaching the kids how to be Godly people. Thank you for encouraging me to write this book and helping in every conceivable way to make it happen, from cooking the recipes while I prepared to take photographs of them to encouraging me when I had difficulty formulating ideas.

You are my dream.

For Hampton, for typing the entire book as I finished writing; for preparing recipes; and for encouraging me.

For Hunter, who is stable and not moved by emotions and helps me to think clearly when my thoughts get muddled; for preparing the recipes, doing research for the health tips and other information in this book; and for helping with the photography

For Graylyn, who stands by my side, cooks with me everyday of my life, and for helping me with the props for the photographs.

For Howlett, who cheers me on, and chops vegetables to perfection; and polishes the silver for the pictures.

For Mary Elizabeth, for always smiling and being sunshine in my day; for prop preparation; and for organizing the cleaning crew.

For Anna Julia, for hugging me and helping me with prop arrangements, and for guarding the food from the cats while I went to get a forgotten item for photographs.

For Milly, who patiently watched and ate the finished product with great enthusiasm.

"And also that every man should eat and drink, and enjoy the good of all his labour, it is the gift of God." Ecclesiastes 3:13

Contents

Introduction

As a law school student and soon to be lawyer, my life seemed to be going in the complete opposite direction than where I have ended up, and boy am I glad! I always wanted to be a mother, but who knew I would be a mother of seven children. I happened to marry an avid hunter and outdoorsman who seemed to have a new creature to be prepared for dinner every other day. As he continued to bring his "catch of the day" home, his butchering and processing of deer, birds, and fish in my clean kitchen quickly became the norm. I wondered how my sister-in-law, Carol, managed in her kitchen. I never have known two brothers who had more of a passion for hunting. Whatever season it happened to be, Scott was going to hunt it. Before we married, and some thereafter, he hunted twice a day! He hunted before and after work and every day of the weekend. Thankfully, he has mellowed and has fantastic relationships with the kids and me. What was a woman who knew nothing about cooking to do with all this wild game and fish? In an attempt to empty my overloaded freezer, I was determined not to purchase any meat from the supermarket for a month. This was extremely challenging in that my husband had cooked most of the game meat that we had eaten up until then. I thought to myself, "Here we go!"

Immediately I began testing recipes, but found it more difficult for me to prepare wild game than the supermarket meat I was accustomed to cooking. I also found that the meat seemed to be dry no matter how I prepared it. I just knew there had to be an easier and better way of preparing this difficult meat and still have a tasty dinner. I knew that our ancestors before us lived by hunting and gathering and could not have eaten tasteless tough meat for every meal.

I began asking everyone I knew about how to prepare venison. Almost everyone told me about marinating the venison in Italian Dressing and wrapping the venison loin in bacon and grilling it. Not that these recipes are bad, I was just looking for something a little more special. I met with several dead ends that month and was disappointed at times but, as I began studying the cuts of meat, and how to extract the best flavors from them, something clicked in my mind and I knew to braise the shoulder and neck of venison, elk, and moose for soups and stews, to brown the loin in a super hot skillet and serve it rare, and that the hindquarter roast was a little more versatile to do a vast amount of recipes. Next I began creating recipes for wild duck, and pheasant. I was surprisingly delighted in the flavor of pheasant after being soaked in wine as the French did with their old birds. These wild birds had more flavor than anything I could find in the supermarket, and they did not really take that much more time to prepare.

With a growing family, I needed to be able to prepare meals that did not afford my being in the kitchen for more than an hour. Amazingly, I found that many of the recipes I created and I am sure my ancestors before me used, took less than thirty minutes to prepare. Now that I discovered the truth about wild game, I rarely had to purchase my animal protein from the grocery store, which helped out tremendously on our finances. These animals seemed to actually have more flavor than supermarket cuts of meat. I also found that some of the tougher cuts of meat ended up having more flavor than the tender cuts. I was truly astounded.

During this process, I had no idea about the health benefits I was giving to my family, until a friend introduced me to a book, *Nourishing Traditions* by

Sally Fallon, that encouraged eating wild game, fish, and fresh-from-the-garden vegetables for maximum health. She states that game meat should be considered health food and is particularly rich in nutrients and minerals. The meat of deer, duck, goose, pheasant, and quail among others is lower in fat and is a great source in B vitamins, zinc, niacin and phosphorus and also has higher omega 3 fatty acids than beef. I knew that most supermarket meats were pumped with unnatural substances,

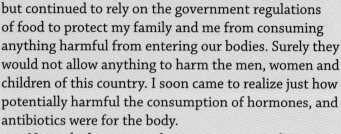

but continued to rely on the government regulations of food to protect my family and me from consuming anything harmful from entering our bodies. Surely they would not allow anything to harm the men, women and children of this country. I soon came to realize just how potentially harmful the consumption of hormones, and antibiotics were for the body.

Not only does most of our meat come with potentially harmful substances, our vegetables do as well. The number of vegetables entering the Genetically Modified category are increasing yearly, not to mention the harmful pesticides being used in the modern farming industry. In that wild game and fish have higher omega three fats, more antioxidants, less fat, and all without the added hormones and antibiotics, how could we go wrong making these proteins our staple foods?

Many people are choosing to take their health into their own hands and have chosen to eat wild, whether they hunt or not. There are many specialty stores and on-line resources where one can purchase any wild game that they would like. Many of these are FDA approved. Some have chosen to become hunters just for the health benefits of the game harvested.

Our children love eating from the wild, in the sense that they feel they are contributing to the family's health and welfare. It truly is a family affair. Every time we sit down for a meal, the kids will comment on the dinner, saying it is the best they have ever eaten. Maybe it really is the best they have eaten or maybe it is just the pride of knowing their contribution to the succulent food on the table. Whatever the cause for the comments, they are getting healthy and they are happy to be at the table with the family. Who could ask for more?

Because of our children's involvement in the harvesting and preparing of the food, they have a great desire to share it with others, especially their grandparents, cousins, and other extended family. This brings about much relationship building and teaches them the importance of hospitality. When their grandparents are proud of them for serving them, the children light up with joy. There is nothing more powerful than food that draws people together, keeps communication open, relationships consistent, and fun and loving than enjoying excellent well prepared, succulent food around a table filled with laughter and joy.

The confidence built through the hunts, the cuisine preparation, the delicious dinners and conversation around the table will not be forgotten. Because of the intensity of the relationships built, children are more likely to make traditions of their own in either hunting, fishing, or just cooking healthy food together for generations to come. One never forgets these experiences, in that dining is an all sensory experience. As the cooks touch the food in preparation of a satiable dinner, aromas fill the house, and laughter and conversation is heard, there is created an anticipation for the eyes to see a beautiful array of fresh vegetables and a lovely presentation of wild game or fish to be tasted with a complete satisfaction and contentment in the enjoyment of life.

My hope for you is that you will become confident in making elegant, succulent dinners for your friends and family and that it would become easy and second nature to use wild game, fish, and vegetables for your main nutrition. I hope it will bring you joy in your relationships and a happier, healthier family. Enjoy getting back to the foods God prepared in a non-altered form for the optimal fuel. Also enjoy the process of hunting, fishing, gathering, or cooking with your loved ones and creating memories for a lifetime.

"He that gathereth in summer is a wise son: but he that sleepeth at harvest is a son that causeth shame." Proverbs 10:5

Starters

Snapper Tartare

Tzatziki with Venison

Turkey Rolls Stuffed with Dates and Goat Cheese

Baked "Fried" Wild Turkey

Duck, Cheese, and Olive Sampler

Bruschetta with Venison, Peppers, Tomatoes, Blue Cheese, and Olive Oil

Timbales

Eggplant Venison Mozzarella Wraps

Indonesian Venison with Peanut Sauce

Quail Lettuce Wraps

Snapper Tartare

Serves 4

Sometimes people are afraid of Tartare believing that the fish is raw. Actually the acid from the lime and orange juices cooks the Snapper. Some folks even like this for a meal and serve the tartare with a salad.

Sharp kitchen scissors dice the fish nicely.

Ingredients

¾ pound very fresh Snapper
Grated zest of 1 lime
3 tablespoons freshly squeezed lime juice
3 tablespoons freshly squeezed orange juice
4 tablespoons olive oil
½ garlic clove
1 ½ teaspoons soy sauce
8 dashes Tabasco sauce
1½ teaspoons of kosher salt
1 teaspoon freshly ground black pepper
¼ cup minced scallions, white and green parts
  (2 scallions)
2 teaspoons minced fresh jalapeno pepper, seeds removed
1 ripe Hass avocado
1 teaspoon toasted sesame seeds

1. Dice snapper into ¼ inch cubes and place in bowl.

2. In a small nonreactive bowl, combine the citrus juices and gently whisk in the olive oil. Add the garlic, soy sauce, Tabasco sauce, salt, and pepper.

3. Pour vinaigrette over the snapper.

4. Cut avocado into ¼ inch cubes. Add avocado, scallions, jalapenos, and sesame seeds. Mix gently but well.

5. Place mixture in refrigerator for one hour.

6. Divide the tartar evenly among four plates. Serve with roasted asparagus on top of the tartar.

Tzatziki with Venison

Serves 8

These bite size starters are a hit at every party. They are just the right size to pick up and eat in a mouthful. This is a tasty, easy appetizer in which the meat can be room temperature and taste fantastic so you can prepare them and plate them before your guest arrive.

Tzatziki	*Venison*
1 large cucumber	**1 lb. venison steaks**
1 cup plain Greek yogurt	**½ teaspoon cinnamon**
3 garlic cloves minced	**¼ teaspoon cumin**
½ cup sour cream	**½ teaspoon cayenne**
3 tablespoons olive oil	**½ teaspoon curry**
4½ teaspoons minced fresh dill	**½ teaspoon ginger**
2 teaspoons red wine vinegar	**Salt**
¼ teaspoon of salt	**Pepper**
Indian Bread 3 x 3 squares	

1. In a medium sized bowl mix cucumbers, yogurt, garlic, sour cream, olive oil, dill, vinegar, and salt.

2. Pound the steaks to ¼ inch thick, slice into ¾ inch strips.

3. In medium sized bowl add cinnamon, cumin, cayenne, curry, ginger, salt, and pepper. Coat venison pieces well.

4. Place venison in smoking hot skillet lightly seasoned with olive oil for 15 to 20 seconds.

5. Cut pita or Indian Bread into squares. Place venison on top of pita squares and top with tzatziki.

Turkey Rolls Stuffed with Dates and Goat Cheese

Serves 6

Goat cheese is one of my very favorite cheeses. The tang of the goat cheese with the sweetness of the date balances excellently with the peppered turkey. These are fabulous.

Cook turkey in small batches, not crowded in the pan. If crowded, the meat will steam instead of brown.

Ingredients
1 lb. wild turkey breast
½ cup fresh goat cheese softened (about 4 oz.)
3 tablespoons heavy cream
18 large dates
Kosher salt
Fresh cracked pepper

1. Slice wild turkey into 1-inch steaks across the grain. Pound them to about ¼ inch thickness. Cut into 1-inch strips about 4 inches long. Salt and pepper both sides.

2. Place the turkey in smoking hot cast iron skillet. Brown turkey until done. This will not take long. Do not overcook. Remove from skillet and let rest.

3. Beat goat cheese by hand until smooth. Stir in heavy cream until mixture is smooth.

4. Slit each date lengthwise and remove pit. Fill each date with goat cheese mixture. Wrap turkey slices around the date and secure with a toothpick.

5. Sprinkle with salt and pepper just before serving.

Baked "Fried" Wild Turkey

Serves 8

I was inspired to create this appetizer when attending an evening wedding of a lifelong friend. It seemed everyone had the chicken fingers with honey mustard sauce and I thought this would work great with wild turkey.

Turkey Ingredients
1 wild turkey breast
1 cup Greek yogurt
3 tablespoons honey
3 cups plain breadcrumbs
Kosher salt
Pepper
Nonstick olive oil spray
Red pepper flakes, to garnish

Sauce Ingredients
¼ cup Dijon mustard
¼ cup Honey
2 tablespoons balsamic vinegar

1. Preheat oven to 425 degrees.

2. Slice turkey breast into ¾ inch slices. Pound to ¼ inch thick with a meat mallet. Slice into 2 inch pieces, the size of chicken fingers. Moderately salt and pepper slices of turkey.

3. Combine yogurt and honey in a medium size bowl. Put breadcrumbs on a separate plate. Dredge turkey pieces in yogurt mixture then coat with breadcrumbs.

4. Place covered turkey slices onto a baking sheet sprayed with nonstick olive oil spray. Coat top of turkey liberally with nonstick olive oil spray. Place in oven for 10 to 15 minutes or until cooked through.

5. Meanwhile, in a small bowl, combine mustard, honey, and balsamic vinegar. Mix well.

6. Remove turkey from oven and place on serving platter. Serve with honey mustard sauce. Garnish with red pepper flakes.

Duck, Cheese, and Olive Sampler

Serves 4

This is one of my very favorite appetizers. The duck is excellently seasoned with the cheeses and olives on crackers. I just cannot get enough of this. The preparation is incredibly easy, and the presentation is beautiful.

Duck meat should always be rare to medium.

At our specialty organic grocery store, I found an extremely knowledgeable cheesemonger that let me taste the cheeses and helped me to decide on my cheese. I chose Cantal French Raw Milk Cheese, goat cheese with dill, and Gouda. At this point, you can use your creativity to compose an incredible dish!

Ingredients

1 8-oz. wild duck breast
2 tablespoons extra-virgin olive oil
Salt and pepper to taste
Platter of goat cheese, cow's raw milk cheese, and Gouda or mozzarella
Salted flat crackers

1. Season the duck breast with salt and pepper.

2. Place duck in smoking hot iron skillet with hot olive oil.

3. Sear until browning begins. This should only take 2½ minutes. Turn over and lightly sear on other side. Do not overcook. Let rest for 5 minutes before slicing.

4. Slice and serve with the cheese and olive platter.

Bruschetta With Venison, Peppers, Tomatoes, Blue Cheese, and Olive Oil

Makes 32 to 36 appetizers

Bruschetta is a great way to use up all kinds of left over vegetables, meats, and cheeses and make delicious hors d'oeuvres at the same time. These savory bites feature some of my favorite flavors from the Mediterranean: fruity olive oil, peppers, capers, and basil, not to mention a little melted Blue Cheese.

Ingredients

1 lb. venison roast
¼ cup olive oil, plus extra for brushing bread
2 red bell peppers, seeded and cut into thin strips
2 yellow bell peppers, seeded and cut into thin strips
1 teaspoon lemon juice
2 tablespoons drained capers
¼ cup julienned fresh basil leaves
Kosher salt and freshly ground black pepper
2 loaves long Baguettes, cut into ½ inch thick
4 to 5 oz. creamy blue cheese, at room temperature

1. Cut venison into 2-inch cubes. Salt and pepper. Sear venison in a very hot cast iron skillet. Brown for approximately 30 seconds each side.

2. Place venison in 350-degree oven, for 4 to 5 minutes or until medium rare. Let rest.

3. Heat olive oil over medium-high heat in a large skillet. Add all the peppers and sauté for 12 to 15 minutes, stirring occasionally until tender. Stir in the capers, basil, and lemon juice, sprinkle with salt and pepper and set aside.

4. Arrange the bread slices in rows on sheet pans. Brush each slice lightly with olive oil and toast for 7 to 10 minutes.

5. Thinly slice the venison.

6. Top each toast with a spoonful of pepper mixture and two slices of venison. Dot each one with blue cheese. Return to oven for two minutes to melt the blue cheese. Sprinkle with salt and serve warm.

Timbales

Serves 4

Timbales are baked custards, seen in the south of France, usually made with vegetables. They can be served warm or cool and they are healthy and delicious.

Ingredients
2 zucchini
2 firm tomatoes, sliced
1 tablespoon tomato sauce
2 tablespoons pesto
2 tablespoons Tabasco
Salt and fresh ground pepper
2 eggs plus 2 egg yolks
3 tablespoons heavy cream
4 tablespoons butter
Kosher salt to taste

1. Preheat oven to 350 degrees.

2. Place sliced zucchini in the microwave with 2 tablespoons of water until steamed. Do not allow to steam too long or you will not be able to handle them. Drain well.

3. Butter ramekin dishes well.

4. Layer zucchini in ramekins alternating with tomatoes. Salt between each layer.

5. Whisk eggs, cream, tomato sauce, pesto, and Tabasco together. Pour carefully into ramekins. Place in roasting pan half filled with hot water for 25 minutes or until custard is slightly firm.

6. Cool slightly. Run a sharp knife around the rim. Turn them out onto a small plate and serve.

Eggplant Venison Mozzarella Wraps

Serves 4

This is a fantastic starter, but with a soup or salad this could be a nice lunch or light dinner.

Ingredients
½ lb. hindquarters
1 large eggplant
8 slices of mozzarella cheese
Olive oil
2 small tomatoes
8 large basil leaves
Balsamic vinegar
Salt and freshly ground pepper

My dad cooks all his meat on the grill on Saturday afternoon. He saves an abundance of time and resources doing this. I have not mastered this yet, but I think it would make life simpler.

1. Cut the eggplant lengthwise. Remove the two outer pieces, only using the 8 pieces. Sprinkle slices with salt and leave them in a colander for 20 minutes.

2. Pre-heat grill on high heat. Slice hindquarter into 8 slices. Pound to ¼ inch. Season with salt and pepper. Brown venison on grill, approximately 30 seconds on each side. Remove and let rest.

3. Rinse eggplant in cold water. Pat dry.

4. Brush slices with oil and grill for 4 minutes on each side.

5. Remove slices from grill. Place mozzarella slice, tomato slice, venison slice, and basil on top of the eggplant. Fold the eggplant over the filling. Place back on grill seam side down until cheese is melted.

6. Serve with balsamic vinegar and olive oil drizzled over the top.

Indonesian Venison With Peanut Sauce

Serves 10

When I make these Indonesian favorites my kids devour them almost before I can put them on the platter. These are great for summer parties such as the 4th of July or Memorial Day. They are so flavorful and the peanut sauce is to die for.

Cut venison while it is still a bit frozen and you will get beautiful thin slices.

Venison Ingredients

1 lb. venison
3 garlic cloves, finely chopped
1 tablespoon medium curry paste
1 teaspoon turmeric
1 teaspoon ground cumin
1 teaspoon grated fresh ginger root
4 tablespoons coconut cream (the thick cream on the top of the coconut milk can)
2 tablespoons Thai fish sauce
1 teaspoon brown sugar
Vegetable oil, for brushing
Red pepper flakes to garnish

Peanut Sauce Ingredients

1 cup coconut milk
½ cup beef stock
3 tablespoons brown sugar
3 oz. crunchy peanut butter
Thai red curry paste
1 tablespoon Thai fish sauce
3 tablespoons tamarind juice
3 tablespoons brown sugar

1. Cut venison to ⅛-inch thick. Pound once with a meat mallet. Place the venison in shallow dish. Mix together the garlic, curry paste, turmeric, cumin, ginger root, coconut cream, fish sauce, and sugar. Pour over the venison and leave to marinate for about 2 hours.

2. Meanwhile, make the sauce. Heat the coconut milk over medium heat, then add beef stock, peanut butter, curry paste, fish sauce, tamarind juice, and brown sugar.

3. Cook stirring constantly, for about 5 to 6 minutes, until smooth. Add salt to taste.

4. Thread meat onto skewers. Brush with oil and cook on a hot grill for 30 seconds on each side, until cooked and golden brown.

5. Serve with the peanut sauce and garnish with red pepper flakes and peanuts.

Quail Lettuce Wraps

Serves 8

There is a restaurant in Birmingham, Alabama that serves fantastic lettuce wraps. I have to get the appetizer every time I go (sometimes 2 of them). The flavors in this recipe totally fulfill my cravings, and I have the pleasure of enjoying them at home.

Ingredients

8 semi-boneless quail
2 tablespoons soy sauce
1 teaspoon red pepper flakes
1 tablespoon hoisin sauce
2 tablespoons lemon juice
¼ cup peanut oil
2 cups diced water chestnuts
½ cup diced white onions
1 cup diced green onions
1 garlic clove smashed
1 tablespoon fresh-smashed ginger
1 tablespoon seasoned rice wine vinegar
3 tablespoons soy sauce
3 tablespoons chicken stock
1 head iceberg lettuce

1. Mix soy sauce, red pepper flakes, hoisin sauce, and lemon juice in casserole. Marinate quail 20 minutes.

2. Grill quail over high heat in a cast iron skillet. Debone quail and cut into small pieces.

3. Heat peanut oil in a wok. Add water chestnuts, white onions, green onions, garlic, and ginger to wok for 2 to 3 minutes.

4. Add vinegar, soy sauce, and chicken stock until caramelized.

5. Place quail in the wok with the onion mixture. Mix well.

6. Serve in lettuce wraps.

"The people asked, and he brought quails, and satisfied them with the bread of heaven." Psalm 105:40

"Go to the ant, though sluggard; consider her ways, and be wise: ...provideth her meat in the summer, and gathereth her food in the harvest." Proverbs 6:6,8

Soups and Salads

Provençal Venison Soup
Soupe au Pistou

Moroccan Stew

Fisherman's Stew

Zucchini Bisque

Homemade Fish Stock

Summer Minestrone

Pumpkin Soup

Easy Vinaigrette

Loquat Vinaigrette

Deer Loin with Arugula, Avocados, and Parmesan Cheese

Fabulous Duck Salad

Summer's Best Tomatoes with Mozzarella and Basil

Black-eyed Peas Salad

Gray's Potato Salad

Homemade Mayonnaise

Cucumber Salad

For our family, soups and salads are a mainstay on the table.

We eat salad or soup at least one meal out of the day. There really is no better way to get the nutrients and a well balanced meal than to have a soup full of fresh vegetables with a protein and to obtain fiber with a salad along side.

Not only are soups and salads so nutritious and balanced, they are a fairly easy "one pot meal". It is nice to have a little break through the day because some days it seems we have just finished breakfast only to start lunch and then lunch to start dinner. Serve the soup with rice and it becomes a hearty meal in itself.

For our family's large size, I usually quadruple the recipe for the soups to save for leftovers or to freeze. I found that the soups do freeze fairly well and it is worth the effort to freeze them especially on those challenging days when dinner time sneaks up on you. If you have the extra hands of children old enough to chop vegetables, you can have them chopping and you will spend half the time in the kitchen... well, maybe.

Provençal Venison Soup
Soupe au Pistou

Serves 8

When I eat this soup I am taken back in time to my sweet granny's quaint kitchen. I have such fond memories of sitting at her table with the plastic tablecloth and the ancient refrigerator within arms reach from the table. She would bring me a grilled cheese sandwich with this perfect vegetable soup and potato salad on the side. It is hard to think of a warmer memory than this. I have used her recipe, but with my twist, adding venison and pesto! How could it get any better than this?

If you need dinner in a hurry and have a pressure cooker, cover the stew meat about 1½ inch with beef stock, onions, and ½ tablespoon of salt. Once the pressure cooker reaches a boil, turn it down to simmer and cook for about 15 minutes. Release the pressure and add to the soup.

Venison Soup Ingredients
1 lb. venison, stew meat
2 garlic cloves, minced
1 tablespoon olive oil
2 onions, minced
1 celery stalk, finely sliced
2 carrots, finely diced
1½ cups butter beans
1½ cups corn
2 small potatoes
2 small zucchini, finely diced
6 tomatoes, peeled, seeded, and finely diced
1 cup shelled or frozen peas
2 quarts water, or just above vegetables
A handful of spinach leaves, cut into thin ribbons
Salt and freshly ground black pepper
Sprigs of fresh basil, to garnish
1 lemon

Pesto Ingredients
2 garlic cloves, minced
1 cup (packed) basil leaves
8 tablespoons grated Parmesan cheese
8 tablespoons extra-virgin olive oil
4 tablespoons pine nuts

1. Place garlic, basil, Parmesan cheese, and pine nuts in a food processor and process until smooth, scraping down the sides once. With the machine running, slowly add the olive oil through the feed tube.

2. In a stew pot, brown venison stew meat. Remove from pot.

3. Heat oil in a large saucepan. Add the onions and cook for 5 minutes, stirring occasionally, until they are beginning to soften.

4. Add butter beans, corn, potatoes, zucchini, tomatoes, peas, and meat to the pot with 2 quarts of water. Bring to a boil then lower to a simmer for one hour or until the vegetables and meat are tender.

5. Add the spinach leaves and cook 5 more minutes. Season with salt and pepper to taste. Add lemon juice of 1 lemon. Serve with pesto and Rustic Bread (p. 164). Garnish with a sprig of basil.

Moroccan Stew

Serves 4

The spices in this dish, with the unique texture of the chickpeas, make for an exciting and surprising soup. I love to have this next to the fire on cold nights after a long day.

Stew Ingredients
1 lb. venison, cut into ½-inch pieces
2 tablespoons butter
1 onion, chopped
1 pint Homemade Canned Tomatoes (p. 154) or 15 oz. can
4 tablespoons chopped fresh cilantro
2 tablespoons chopped fresh parsley
½ teaspoon turmeric
½ teaspoon ground cinnamon
¼ cup red kidney beans
½ cup chickpeas
2½ cups water
½ cup onions, diced
Salt and freshly-ground black pepper

Garnish Ingredients
Chopped fresh cilantro
Lemon slices

1. Heat the butter in a large stockpot. Brown venison and onions for 5 minutes.

2. Quarter the tomatoes and add to the venison. Add the water, cilantro, parsley, beans, turmeric, and cinnamon.

3. Add red kidney beans and chickpeas. Season with salt and pepper and bring to a boil. Simmer for 1½ hours. Garnish with cilantro and lemon slices.

Fisherman's Stew

Serves 4

There is nothing like the combination of flavors of fish, bacon, and onions stewed in white wine to wake the taste buds.

Ingredients

6 slices good quality bacon without nitrates
1 tablespoon butter
2 garlic cloves, minced
1½ large onions
2 tablespoons chopped fresh parsley
1 teaspoon fresh thyme leaves or ½ teaspoon dried thyme
4 cups peeled, seeded, and chopped tomatoes
   or 1 28 oz. can plum tomatoes, diced
⅔ cup vermouth or white wine
2½ cups Homemade Fish Stock (p. 47)
2 cups diced potatoes
2 lbs. skinless flounder fillets, cut into large chunks
kosher salt and freshly ground black pepper
Fresh flat leaf parsley, to garnish
½ lemon

1. Fry the bacon in a large saucepan over medium heat until light brown, but not crisp. Remove from the pan and drain on paper towels.

2. Melt the butter in the pan with the bacon fat. Add the onions and cook, stirring occasionally, for 3 to 5 minutes or until soft. Add the garlic and herbs and continue cooking for 1 minute, stirring constantly. Add the tomatoes, vermouth or wine, and stock and bring to a boil.

3. Lower the heat, cover, and simmer the stew for 15 minutes. Add the potatoes, cover again, and simmer for 10 to 12 minutes longer or until the potatoes are almost tender.

4. Add the chunks of fish and the bacon strips. Simmer, uncovered, for 5 minutes, or until the fish is just cooked and the potatoes are tender. Season with salt and pepper. Squeeze the juice of ½ lemon to add brightness. Garnish with flat leaf parsley.

Homemade Fish Stock

Ingredients

**3 carcasses, including heads of non-oily fish such as
  Snapper, Flounder, or Tilapia**
2 tablespoons olive oil
2 carrots, unpeeled and chopped
½ cups yellow onions
4 stalks celery, chopped
2 cloves garlic
5 sprigs fresh thyme
3 sprigs parsley
½ cup good white wine
Kosher salt
1½ teaspoon freshly ground black pepper
2 quarts water

After you have removed the congealed fat, you can freeze fish stock in ice cube trays then transfer the fish stock ice cubes to freezer bags for long term storage.

1. Warm oil in stockpot. Add carrots, onions, and celery over medium heat for about 15 minutes, or until lightly browned. Add garlic and cook for 2 more minutes.

2. Add fish carcasses, water, white wine, salt, pepper, thyme, and parsley to the pot. Bring to a boil and reduce heat to a simmer for about 3 hours.

3. Remove carcasses with tongs and strain the liquid. Place in refrigerator and remove any congealed fat before use.

Zucchini Bisque

Serves 6

We planted way too many zucchini in our garden a few years ago, and in an attempt not to waste any, I made a huge batch of zucchini soup. The soup was so light and creamy, I knew this would be a new favorite staple food in our home for years to come.

Ingredients
1 tablespoon unsalted butter
1 tablespoon good olive oil
2 onions
5 cups chopped leeks (4 to 8 leeks), white and
**   light green parts**
12 Yukon potatoes
3 zucchini
1½ quarts Homemade Chicken Stock (p. 95)
**   or canned stock**
1 teaspoon kosher salt
½ teaspoon freshly ground black pepper
¼ cup heavy cream
Fresh chives

Depending on your taste, you may like a thick creamy soup or a looser soup. Add more broth if it seems too thick or add a few more potatoes if it seems to loose.

1. Heat butter and oil in large stockpot. Add onions and leeks over medium heat until onions are translucent (about 5 minutes).

2. Add zucchini, potatoes, stock, salt, and pepper. Bring to a boil. Lower heat and simmer for ½ an hour.

3. If you have an emulsion blender, blend ingredients right in the stockpot. If not, transfer soup to a food processor and puree. Return soup back to pot. Add cream and season to taste. Garnish with chives.

Summer Minestrone

Serves 4

This is truly a beautiful soup. The bright, roughly-chopped vegetables are great for an outdoor lunch with family or friends.

Ingredients
3 tablespoons olive oil
1 tablespoon butter
1 large onion, minced
1 tablespoon tomato paste
2 zucchini, roughly chopped
4 yellow squash, trimmed roughly
3 cups peeled and chopped ripe Italian plum tomatoes or
 28 oz. can plum tomatoes
3 waxy new potatoes, diced
2 garlic cloves, crushed
1¼ quarts vegetable stock or water
4 tablespoons shredded fresh basil
⅔ cup grated Parmesan cheese
Salt and freshly ground black pepper

1. Heat the oil in a large stockpot and add the onion and cook on low until translucent.

2. Stir the tomato paste, yellow squash, zucchini, plum tomatoes, new potatoes, and garlic into the stockpot. Simmer for 5 minutes, taking care not to allow vegetable to stick to the bottom of the stockpot.

3. Pour in the stock or water and bring to a boil. Lower the heat and simmer for 25 minutes, or until the vegetables are just tender. Add more stock if necessary.

4. Remove the stockpot from the heat and stir in the basil and half the cheese. Taste and adjust the seasoning. Garnish with remaining cheese.

Pumpkin Soup

Serves 4

Pumpkin is another nutritious, creamy, and elegant soup. It is similar to zucchini bisque but has an earthier, nuttier flavor. This is a great soup to serve as a starter during the Thanksgiving and Christmas holidays.

Ingredients
3 tablespoons butter
2 large onions, minced
4½ cups peeled, seeded, and cubed pumpkin
2 quarts Homemade Chicken Stock (p. 95) or canned broth
2 cups cubed Idaho potatoes
½ teaspoon paprika
⅓ cup whipping cream (optional)
1½ tablespoons snipped fresh chives, plus a few whole chives to garnish
Salt and freshly ground back pepper

1. Melt the butter in a large stockpot. Add the onions and cook until translucent.

2. Add the pumpkin, stock, potatoes, and paprika and bring to a boil. Lower the heat to simmer, cover the stockpot for about 35 minutes, or until all the vegetables are soft.

3. Blend ingredients with an emulsion blender or transfer to a food processor and puree. Return to stockpot. Add whipping cream. Season with salt and pepper.

4. Stir in the chopped chives just before serving. Garnish each serving with a few whole chives.

The best way to separate the flesh from the outer layer of the pumpkin is to cut the pumpkin in half, then cut it into slices about 2 inches thick. Cut the flesh from the outer layer and then proceed to make 1-inch cubes.

Easy Vinaigrette

The very best dressing for any salad is a simple vinaigrette dressing. These dressings are extremely versatile to fit the salad being served. Vinaigrettes are merely an emulsion of oil, acid, and fresh herbs. They are extremely healthy and add tremendous flavors to the lettuce or spinach leaves or an array of green herbs.

Store vinaigrette for up to one week in an airtight container in refrigerator.

Olive oil supplies us with many antioxidants and vitamin E as well as protects from heart disease. Vinegar or lemon juice, or sometimes orange juice, supply our bodies with enzymes that aid in the digestion of food. These well-balanced flavors and healthful benefits should always be an accompaniment to any salad.

Ingredients

1½ cups olive oil
¼ cup lemon juice
½ teaspoon fresh garlic, minced
½ teaspoon Dijon mustard
1 teaspoon salt
½ teaspoon black pepper

Place lemon juice, garlic, mustard, salt, and pepper into a medium-sized bowl. Slowly pour olive oil into mixture, while continuously whisking as to ensure an emulsion.

Loquat Vinaigrette

Ingredients
2 cups red wine vinegar
½ cup honey
1½ teaspoons hot red pepper flakes
1 teaspoon black peppercorns
15 loquats or ¼ lb. loquats thinly sliced
1 cup extra virgin olive oil
Kosher salt and freshly ground black pepper

The vinaigrette goes great with duck, quail, and pheasant dishes.

1. In medium saucepan, combine vinegar, honey, red pepper flakes, and peppercorns. Cook over medium-high heat until reduced by two thirds.

2. Place loquats in a shallow casserole and pour mixture over them. Let stand 1 hour.

3. Place mixture in food processor and puree. Slowly drizzle in the olive oil whisking constantly to form an emulsion. Season with salt and pepper.

Deer Loin with Arugula, Avocados, and Parmesan Cheese

Serves 4

What is much better than perfectly prepared venison loin over slightly bitter arugula with delicious simple vinaigrette dressing only to be topped off with shaved Parmesan cheese and creamy avocados? It is a meal in itself.

Ingredients
1 venison loin
¼ cup good olive oil, for brushing onto loin
kosher salt and pepper
Easy vinaigrette (p.54)
8 oz. baby arugula
1 4 oz. chunk good Parmesan cheese

1. Preheat oven to 250 degrees.
2. Brush olive oil onto loin then salt and pepper the loin. Brown loin on all sides in a super hot cast iron skillet. Place loin in oven for 5 minutes. Remove and let rest.
3. Make Easy Vinaigrette (p. 54)
4. Remove avocados from the shell and remove pits. Cut avocados into 1-inch slices.
5. With a vegetable peeler, slice Parmesan cheese in long, thin pieces.
6. Toss arugula in large bowl with enough dressing to moisten. Divide among 4 plates. Place venison loin, avocados, and cheese among each plate. Sprinkle with salt and serve immediately.

Fabulous Duck Salad

Serves 6

The first time I had this wonderful salad Scott and I were on our honeymoon in Jackson Hole, Wyoming. I think I have replicated this salad pretty close to the best of my memory.

Ingredients

2 wild duck breast
½ teaspoon kosher salt
1 tablespoon minced red onion
2½ tablespoons champagne vinegar
½ cup good olive oil
1 teaspoon grated orange zest
4 cups mixed greens with baby arugula
3 oranges, peeled, and sectioned
½ pint blueberries
½ pint fresh raspberries
1 cup toasted whole pecan halves

Marinade

1 teaspoon salt
½ teaspoon pepper
½ cup olive oil
1 clove of garlic, crushed,
1 tablespoon fresh thyme

1. Mix salt, pepper, garlic, olive oil, and thyme in a casserole. Place the duck breast in marinade for 1 or more hours if you have time.

2. Heat a dry saucepan. Cook pecans over low heat for about five minutes. Stir often and do not leave the stove. They burn quickly, as I know from experience.

3. Combine onion, vinegar, orange zest, and salt in a small bowl. Whisk in olive oil.

4. Place marinated duck into a dry smoking hot skillet and brown for 3 minutes per side. Remove from skillet and let rest.

5. In a large salad bowl, mix mixed greens, oranges, blueberries, raspberries, and pecans. Pour dressing into bowl and gently toss.

6. Thinly slice duck breast and place on salad. Serve immediately.

Summer's Best Tomatoes with Mozzarella and Basil

Serves 8

One of my best friends from Tuscaloosa, Alabama surprised me with this dish when she and her husband, John Kelley, were delivering a painting to my home. He happens to be my second favorite artist (Scott is my first). I just loved the fresh simple flavors of the tomatoes and basil with the creamy mozzarella. The drizzle of olive oil and balsamic vinegar really brighten the entire dish.

Ingredients
6 medium tomatoes
1 lb. fresh mozzarella
15 basil leaves
5 tablespoons good olive oil
3 tablespoons balsamic vinegar
Kosher salt
Freshly ground black pepper

1. On a platter, alternate tomatoes, mozzarella, and basil leaves. Drizzle balsamic vinegar and olive oil over the vegetables.
2. Sprinkle with salt and pepper.

Black-eyed Peas Salad

Serves 8

This is lovely for winter or summer. It is not only colorful, but it is full of flavor. Black-eyed peas grow profusely in the south and freeze very well.

Ingredients

3 cups fresh or frozen black-eyed peas
1 tablespoon kosher salt
½ tablespoon freshly ground black pepper
1 large red onion
2 tomatoes, diced (¾ cup)
2 tablespoons cilantro, coarsely chopped
1 garlic cloves, minced
1 teaspoon Dijon mustard
Juice of 1 lemon
6 tablespoons extra-virgin olive oil
10 cups baby spinach

1. In a stockpot, bring 4 cups of water, salt, pepper, and the peas to a boil. Once the peas reach a boil, lower to a simmer for 30 minutes or until the peas are just done. Let cool.

2. In a large bowl gently mix black-eyed peas, red onions, tomatoes, cilantro, garlic, mustard, lemon juice, and olive oil.

3. Mix spinach gently into black-eyed pea mixture. Serve at room temperature.

Gray's Potato Salad

Serves 6

This is the potato salad my granny used to make to go as a side with her famous vegetable soup. I have tweaked this recipe several times and always revert back to her original potato salad. It really cannot be improved.

Ingredients

8 small new potatoes, boiled
2 boiled eggs
4 Vidalia onions, minced
½ cup dill pickles
½ cup mayonnaise
2 tablespoons Dijon mustard
3 celery stalks, minced
1 tablespoon kosher salt
1 teaspoon pepper

1. Cut the new potatoes into four pieces roughly 1½-inch pieces. There is no need to remove the skin. Place the potatoes into medium saucepan and boil until a knife will easily go through the still-firm potatoes.

2. Meanwhile, in a medium-sized bowl add the onions, pickles, mayonnaise, mustard, celery, salt, and pepper.

3. Drain potatoes until they appear to be dry and place them in a bowl with the mayonnaise mixture.

4. Place chopped boiled eggs onto potatoes. Mix gently (I use my hands) so as not to crush the potatoes. Serve hot or cold. Garnish with parsley.

Homemade Mayonnaise (p. 67) always beats store bought mayonnaise, but if you do not have time, Hellman's is a great mayonnaise to use instead.

Homemade Mayonnaise

Yields approximately 1 pint

It seems every time I need mayonnaise, I cannot find a drop in the house. Instead of going to the grocery store I began making a recipe that I was given for homemade mayonnaise and surprisingly it only took five minutes and it tasted so fresh, bright and just plain GREAT.

Ingredients
1 egg
2 egg yolks
1 teaspoon Dijon mustard
1½ tablespoons Meyer lemon juice
½ teaspoon salt
¼ teaspoon white pepper
2 cups olive oil

1. In a food processor add egg, egg yolks, lemon juice, mustard, salt, and white pepper.

2. Start food processor and run continuously while very slowly adding drops of oil waiting 30 seconds between each drop. Continue with the drops for about ¼ cup of oil.

3. When mayonnaise has definitely thickened add oil in a stream. You may not need all the oil at this time therefore check after each ½ cup is added for thickness and taste. If the consistency of mayonnaise is very thick, add a drop of lemon to thin it or if too thin add more oil.

4. Place mayonnaise in a bowl and serve or keep covered in refrigerator for one week.

Never use aluminum bowls or saucepans to prepare mayonnaise, as they will turn the mayonnaise gray. Also store it in plastic, glass, or stainless steel as well.

Use the freshest available eggs possible.

All ingredients must be at room temperature.

Cucumber Salad

Serves 10

My mother in-law is a great cook and I have learned so much from her. She introduced me to this wonderful recipe for which I have found so many uses. It is excellent over warm fish.

Ingredients
4 cucumbers (approximately 4 cups), diced
1 large squash
3 tablespoons fresh basil, chopped
¼ cup salad vinegar
2 tablespoons olive oil
1 tablespoon sugar
¼ teaspoon salt
¼ pepper
5 tomatoes (4 cups, diced)
½ Vidalia onion

1. Mix well vinegar, oil, sugar, salt, and pepper in salad bowl.

2. Peel cucumbers and trim ends. Cut cucumbers lengthwise. Scrape out the seeds with a spoon, dice, and place cucumber pieces in the salad bowl.

3. Dice tomatoes, squash, and onions and place in bowl with cucumbers. Add basil and mix well.

Dinners

Venison Bourguignon

Stuffed Venison Loin

Venison Enchiladas

Parmesan Venison

Venison, Roasted Peppers, and Goat Cheese Sandwiches

Venison Sliders

Wild Turkey Piccata

Wild Turkey Chili

Basic Pie Crust

Turkey Pot Pie

Homemade Chicken Stock

Whole Bass with Tomatoes

Fabulous Bream

Roasted Snapper with Mustard Sauce

Spicy Scamp with Roasted Vegetables

Trout in Papillote

Duck Breast with Figs and Mushrooms

Goose Siciliana

Wild Duck with Hash Browns and Eggs

Provençal Quail over Grits

Grilled Quail with Caramelized Peaches

Coq au Vin Pheasant Style

Countryside Pheasant

"Now therefore take, I pray thee, thy weapons, thy quiver and thy bow, and go out to the field, and take me some venison; and make me savoury meat such as I love that I may eat…" Genesis 27: 3-4

I think all men were created to take dominion.

In having boys and girls, there seems to be prevalent "gene " in boys to dominate, lead, and a want to control. I love to see this energy released in the preparation, strategizing, planning, and harvesting of their game. I love to see their mental and physical energies used in this worthwhile, and productive venture during these developing years. I have never heard the boys complain about having to work on the farm to prepare for the hunts. They seem to live for it! The only activity that comes close to my men's love for hunting is preparing the land for hunting.

I love to see Scott enjoying teaching all the skills and knowledge of hunting he has developed through the years with the kids. Not only do I love this for the boys, I love this release of energy for Scott. It is a great stress reliever after a week of dentistry. As much as he loves his patients, he needs a passionate diversion that uses his mental and physical energy in a more expansive place. I find land is limitless in its size and usefulness and Scott loves to work the land and use it to the fullest possibility. I have never seen anyone more passionate about land and hunting than Scott. He overwhelms me with his passion and creativity in this arena. I find that all the hard physical work involved in preparing the land and all the thought he puts into the planning of it recreates him as a person, and the joy of it all is that he gets to experience it all with his best buddies, his kids. He is investing in the future by building relationships that last for a lifetime.

The word venison *applies to all meat from deer including but not limited to whitetail deer, mule deer, elk, moose, and caribou.*

The girls do join Scott as well in these hunts and the shooting range and are nearly as knowledgeable as the boys in land management and deer harvesting. The girls cheer their dad and brothers on as they harvest there game as do the boys for the girls. I love hearing them talk about where they think the deer are going to appear and the strategy for their hunts. When hunting season comes to a close, they immediately begin planning for the next season. It seems that there is always room for improvement and experimentation year after year. They never tire of this awesome, challenging, and rewarding pursuit.

Venison Bourguignon

Serves 6

This dish is one of my easy standbys on days I do not know what we are having for dinner. Scott and the kids devour it and it is great for winter nights. This dish is also so full of flavor that I often use it when entertaining guests.

In France this dish is often served on top of crusty bread. It is delicious this way.

Make sure venison is dry when you brown it. If it is not dry it will steam the meat instead of browning it.

Ingredients

3 lbs. venison stew meat or hindquarter, cut into 1 inch pieces
2 tablespoons good olive oil
8 oz. good bacon, diced
Kosher salt
Freshly ground black pepper
4 large Vidalia onions
4 carrots, sliced diagonally into 1-inch chunks
2 teaspoons chopped garlic (2 cloves)
2½ cups canned beef broth
2 cups good red wine
1 tablespoon tomato paste
2 teaspoons fresh thyme leaves
3 tablespoons all-purpose flour
4 tablespoons (½ stick) unsalted butter at room temperature, divided
1 lb. mushrooms, thickly sliced

1. Heat the olive oil in a large Dutch oven or stockpot over medium-heat. Add the bacon and cook over medium heat for 8 to 10 minutes, or until the bacon is lightly browned. Remove the bacon with a slotted spoon.

2. Salt and pepper venison. In very hot skillet add a single layer of venison, brown it on all sides working in batches. Do not crowd the pan or the meat will steam instead of brown. Set aside.

3. Place onions, and carrots into the stockpot. Cook over medium-heat for approximately 10 minutes or until the onions are lightly browned. Add garlic and cook for one minute longer. Add the wine and broth into pot. Add the venison, bacon, tomato paste, and thyme. Bring to a boil. When it reaches a boil turn it to low and simmer for about 1½ hours.

4. Sauté mushrooms in 2 tablespoons of butter until lightly browned. Add to stew.

5. Thicken the stew by mixing ¼ cup of water, 2 tablespoons of flour, and 2 tablespoons of butter. Pour mixture into pot. Simmer for about 5 minutes.

6. Garnish with parsley and serve with crusty bread and butter.

Stuffed Venison Loin

Serves 8

This is my family's favorite Christmas dinner. It is an elegant dish that melts in your mouth and is lovely for holidays and special occasions. The cheese and herbs make this dish rich and flavorful.

Ingredients

2 venison loins, butterflied
½ cup breadcrumbs
¾ cup shredded mozzarella cheese
1 cup Parmesan cheese
½ cup olive oil
½ cup chopped basil leaves
2 garlic cloves, minced
Salt
Pepper

1. In a medium sized bowl, mix together breadcrumbs, cheeses, olive oil, basil, and garlic.

2. Pre-heat oven to 350 degrees. Butterfly the two loins.

3. Spread filling evenly over the loin. Roll up the loin and truss.

4. Liberally sprinkle with salt and pepper. Place in smoking hot cast iron skillet. Brown loins on all sides. Place loins in 350-degree oven for 3 to 4 minutes. Remove from pan. Let rest. Slice into 1-inch pieces. Serve with Homemade Mashed Potatoes (p. 150), rice, carrots, green beans, or salad.

How To Butterfly a Loin

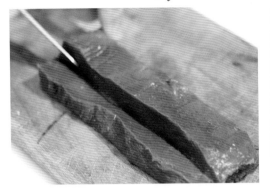

With a long sharp knife on the right half of the loin, slice loin ⅔ of the way through.

Turn the loin over and repeat.

Spread sliced loin out.

Pound the loin to about ¼ inch thick and spread stuffing on top.

Roll loin and begin to truss.

How To Truss a Loin

Using butchers twine about 6 times longer than your loin, wrap around loin approximately 1½ inches from end and tie a knot.

Hold the short end of the twine above the knot with your left hand. Pull the long end of the twine away from you and slip it under the part of the twine that you are holding taut above the loin. Repeat wrapping process every 1½ to 2 inches until entire loin is trussed.

Turn the loin over and stretch the twine around the end, wrapping around each truss until it reaches the first initial truss. Tie ends together and trim excess.

Venison Enchiladas

Serves 8

The first time Anna Julia ate this she exclaimed, "this is the best thing I ever ated." Enough said!

Ingredients

2 lbs. venison hindquarter, pounded, and cut into 1- by 2-inch pieces
2 medium garlic cloves, minced
3 tablespoons chili powder
2 teaspoons cumin
2 teaspoons coriander
1 tablespoon kosher salt
1 tablespoons olive oil
2 bell pepper, chopped
2 medium onions, chopped
4 cups Basic Tomato Sauce (p. 155)
   or 30 oz. can tomato sauce
2 cups water
3 cups Monterey Jack cheese
1 cup cilantro
¼ cup jalapenos, chopped
8 6-inch corn tortillas *

Store the filling in airtight containers in the freezer for up to 3 months. You can also store the tortillas separately from the filling by placing parchment paper between each tortilla and storing them in a zip top bag and freezing them. Place in the microwave on ½ power for 10 to 20 seconds.

1. Mix garlic, chili powder, cumin, coriander, and salt in a small bowl.

2. Cut hindquarter into 2-inch pieces. Pound to ¼ inch thick. Cut into 1- by 2-inch pieces.

3. Dredge meat in spice mixture and shake off excess. In Dutch oven or large pot heat oil until smoking hot. Brown venison 30 seconds on each side. Transfer to cooling rack and set aside.

4. Reduce heat on same pot and add peppers and onions until golden. Stir in remaining chili powder cumin mixture and cook for about 1 minute. Add tomato sauce and water and bring to a boil. Simmer for 30 minutes.

5. Place in 13- x 9-inch casserole just enough sauce from the pot to cover bottom of casserole.

6. Return meat back to pot along with 2 cups of cheese, cilantro, and jalapenos.

7. Warm tortillas about 1 minute in microwave to make it pliable. Place approximately 1/3 cup of meat mixture down the middle of each tortilla. Wrap them and place them seam side down in casserole. Some may have to be placed down the side of the casserole. Pour remaining sauce over enchiladas and spread evenly. Sprinkle remaining cheese over enchiladas and wrap with aluminum foil and place in 350-degree oven for 20 minutes. Remove foil and continue baking until cheese is slightly brown. Serve with rice.

Parmesan Venison

Serves 6

When serving a large amount of people, preheat the oven to 225 degrees. Put cooked venison on a cooling rack on top of a cookie sheet and place in oven while the remaining venison is being prepared.

If you want to make a double batch and have leftovers, seal in an airtight container and leave in refrigerator. When ready to use, preheat oven to 225 degrees and place venison in oven for about 15 minutes or until warmed through. It will retain its crispy outer texture.

This recipe is a staple in my home. The crispy coating with the decadent venison pairs beautifully with homemade Basic Tomato Sauce (p. 155) and a salad dressed in tangy Easy Vinaigrette (p. 54).

Ingredients

1½ lbs. venison loin
2 cups all purpose flour
2 teaspoons kosher salt
1 teaspoon freshly ground black pepper
3 extra large eggs
2 cups breadcrumbs, dried, and seasoned
1 cup freshly grated Parmesan cheese, plus
 extra for serving

1. Slice venison into 1-inch pieces. Pound to ¼ inch thick.

2. In a plate, mix together flour, salt, and pepper. On a second plate, beat the eggs with 1 tablespoon of water. On a third plate, mix breadcrumbs and Parmesan cheese.

3. Lightly dredge venison in the flour mixture, then the egg wash, and then the Parmesan breadcrumb mixture.

4. Heat oil and butter in large cast iron skillet or sauté pan. Cook for about 2 minutes over medium heat on each side or until browned. Place pieces on cooling rack.

5. Place each piece of venison on a plate and serve with Basic Tomato Sauce (p. 155) or your favorite marinara sauce.

Venison, Roasted Peppers, and Goat Cheese Sandwiches

Serves 6

The last time I made this for our family, my poor, sweet husband did not get one bite. He was busy outside on the tractor and everyone thought he had already eaten and they finished it off. He was very disappointed, but I made another one just for him later that evening. The lemon juice really adds bright freshness to this sandwich.

Sandwich Ingredients
2 yellow bell peppers
1 red bell pepper
1 Vidalia onion
2 lbs. venison loin
Kosher salt
Pepper
2 French baguettes 20 inches long
12 oz. goat cheese
2 oz. Parmesan cheese, shaved
Arugula

For Marinade
3 tablespoons olive oil
2 garlic cloves, minced
1½ tablespoons lemon juice
2 teaspoons kosher salt
1 teaspoon pepper

1. Preheat oven to 500 degrees. Place peppers in oven for 45 minutes or until skin is charred. Remove from oven and cover until they are cool enough to handle. Remove skin. Slice down the middle and remove seeds and stems. Slice into ½-inch slices.

2. Slice onion in circles. Set aside.

3. Mix oil, garlic, lemon juice, salt, and pepper in medium sized bowl. Add roasted peppers to the mixture for 15 minutes.

4. Preheat oven to 350 degrees. Salt and pepper venison loin. Over high heat sear all sides for 2 minutes per side or until browned. Place in oven for 5 minutes. Remove and let rest.

5. Slice baguette down the center lengthwise. Spread goat cheese onto the bottom of the baguette.

6. Slice venison thinly and place on top of goat cheese. Place pepper mixture on top of venison. Add onions, arugula, and shaved Parmesan on top. Place top piece of bread on sandwich. Serve immediately.

Use a vegetable peeler to make beautiful long pieces of Parmesan cheese.

Venison Sliders

Serves 6

Sliders are once again in vogue. They are fabulous small burgers that are fun to eat for everyone, especially kids. In that you usually eat more than one, you can have two completely different burgers to satisfy all your creative taste.

It is really fun to add good bacon without nitrates, red onions, avocados, or any great accompaniment to a slider and allow everyone to build their own.

Ingredients

**2 lbs. ground venison mixed with 10% beef fat
  (I like the taste and texture without the fat)**
1 onion, minced
5 tablespoons good olive oil
2 tablespoons Dijon mustard
1 tablespoon garlic, minced (3 cloves)
2 teaspoons chopped fresh thyme leaves
1 teaspoon kosher salt
½ teaspoon pepper
6 oz. your favorite cheese
2 long French baguettes
4 red tomatoes, sliced
Baby arugula
Homemade Mayonnaise (p. 67)
Good ketchup, for serving

1. Prepare a grill, or griddle to medium high heat.

2. Put 90% ground venison and 10% ground beef in a bowl and mix.

3. Add minced onion, garlic, oil, mustard, thyme, salt, and pepper into the ground meat. Mix gently. Divide mixture in half and then divide each half into 12 patties.

4. Place burgers on grill and cook 6 minutes per side without moving them too often. Place cheese on the burgers and close lid if cooking on a grill or cover with a bowl if on the griddle to melt the cheese. Remove burgers to large plate or platter. Let rest.

5. Cut baguettes into 24 1-inch slices and toast on grill.

6. Place each burger on top of toasted baguette slices with a slice of tomato and arugula. Cover with other slice. Serve with Homemade Mayonnaise and good ketchup.

We recently acquired a baby turkey

that is now our new best friend. This turkey follows us all over the yard like a loyal dog. We feed it the crickets we find in the grass and as you can see it is eager to be fed this delicacy!

Turkey hunting has become a few of my boy's favorite game to hunt. Some days the hunts can be fairly quick when the turkeys respond to well developed calling techniques which we practice all year! The beauty of the rising sun seems new every time they go. It is amazing that these one sighted dominion takers never cease to tell me of the colorful sunrise. I guess they are not all that one sighted after all.

Scott finds it challenging to hunt turkeys with his recurve bow, which I find impossible! When he does not use his bow, he uses his smooth bore fowling musket that he built especially for turkey hunting. He finds great pleasure in creating these guns and then using them to obtain awesome meat for the family. He makes flint-lock rifles for deer hunting which can be quite challenging if hunting in the rain. Disappointment arises if he sees a huge buck and his gun does not fire because the powder got wet!

Scott started the boys turkey hunting when they could barely walk and I think that was very wise considering you do not have to stay in the woods all day. I think this will be a favorite season of mine for years to come.

Wild Turkey Piccata

Serves 4

The flavors of the wine, capers, olive oil, and wild turkey are perfectly pleasing and balanced. This is one of my all time favorite comfort foods. Piccata is a favorite staple among Italians.

Ingredients
1 wild turkey breast
1 cup flour
1 teaspoon kosher salt
½ teaspoon pepper
2 eggs
1 tablespoon water
1 cup breadcrumbs
1 tablespoon unsalted butter, cold
Olive oil
½ cup wine
2 tablespoons capers
2 tablespoons fresh thyme leaves or
  ½ teaspoon dried

1. Cut turkey breast into ¾ inch pieces. Pound to ¼ inch thick with a meat mallet.

2. On a large plate mix flour, salt, and pepper. On a second plate beat eggs and water together. On a third plate place breadcrumbs. Dredge pounded turkey breast pieces into seasoned flour mix, then egg mixture, then breadcrumbs.

3. In a hot sauté pan, melt butter and oil. When sizzling, place turkey in pan and brown for about 2 minutes per side. Cook in batches. Do not crowd the pan. Transfer to a platter and keep warm.

4. Pour wine, capers, and thyme into the pan. Bring to a boil. Reduce by one third. Add the cold butter.

5. Place the turkey pieces on platter, pour caper sauce over the meat, and serve.

Wild Turkey Chili

Serves 6

I do not know anyone who does not love chili. This is one of our family's favorite turkey recipes. There are so many different variations to this dish and it is always a winner no matter which variation you choose. We love to add corn, avocados, rice, or chips to this dish. Our favorite is just to add the jalapenos, a little cheese and a dollop of sour cream.

Ingredients

4 tablespoons olive oil
2 lbs. wild ground turkey
1½ large onion, chopped
1 red bell pepper, chopped
1 yellow bell pepper, chopped
2 cans dark red kidney beans, rinsed and drained
1 can light kidney beans, rinsed and drained
1 quart tomatoes, chopped or 2 15 oz. cans of chopped tomatoes
1 quart Homemade Chicken Stock (p. 95) or canned broth
3 tablespoons tomato paste
4 tablespoons chili powder
2½ tablespoons ground cumin
¾ teaspoon salt
½ teaspoon freshly ground black pepper
Juice of 1 lemon
2 jalapenos
2 cups shredded cheese
Sour cream

1. In large stockpot heat olive oil. Cook turkey, onions, and peppers over medium-high heat stirring often until the turkey is browned and fully cooked.

2. Add beans, tomatoes with their juices, chicken stock, tomato paste, chili powder, cumin, salt, pepper, and juice of 1 lemon to the stockpot with the turkey mixture. Mix well. Simmer for 1 hour. Add liquid if it seems too dry. Serve with sliced jalapenos, cheese, and sour cream.

Homemade Chicken Stock

Makes 6 quarts

Whole free range chickens may be found in oriental markets. They may have the feet and head still attached which has excellent flavor and gelatin.

Ingredients

3 5-lb. whole free range roasting chickens
3 large yellow onions, unpeeled, quartered
6 carrots, unpeeled, halved
4 celery stalks with leaves, cut in thirds
20 sprigs fresh parsley
15 sprigs fresh thyme
20 sprigs fresh dill
1 head garlic, unpeeled, cut in half crosswise
2 tablespoons kosher salt
2 teaspoons whole black peppercorns

1. Cut chickens into several pieces. Place chicken, carrots, onions, celery stalks, parsley, dill, thyme, garlic, salt, and pepper in large stockpot. Add 7 quarts of water. Bring to a boil and simmer for 6 hours. Turn burner off and let it sit for 1 hour. Strain.

2. Place chicken stock in refrigerator overnight. The next day remove surface fat. Use immediately or freeze for up to 3 months.

Turkey Pot Pie

Serves 8

On a cold winter night, I love to have this creamy, filling comfort food while sitting around the fire laughing and talking with Scott and the kids. This casual food represents coziness and tranquility.

Make a double batch of filling and freeze it. If in a pinch use a store bought Pillsbury crust and you will have a healthful quick dinner.

This recipe can also be adapted by using any leftover vegetables in your refrigerator. It might not taste exactly the same, but it will still be creamy and fantastic.

Ingredients For Meat
3 lbs. wild turkey
3 tablespoons olive oil
Kosher salt and freshly ground black pepper

Filling Ingredients
5 cups Homemade Chicken Stock (p. 95)
2 tablespoons salt
1½ sticks butter, plus extra for seasoning ramekin dishes
2 cups Vidalia onions (2 onions), chopped
¾ cup all-purpose flour
¼ cup heavy cream
**2 cups medium carrots (4 carrots), diced, blanched for
  2 minutes**
1 10 oz. package frozen peas (2 cups)
½ cup fresh parsley, minced

1. Preheat oven to 375 degrees. Slice turkey breast into 1-inch thick slices. Pound turkey to ¼ inch thickness. Salt and pepper turkey on both sides. In a super hot cast iron skillet pour olive oil and place pounded turkey and brown about 2 minutes per side. Set aside.

2. In a large saucepan, melt butter and sauté onions over medium high heat for 10 minutes or until translucent. Add flour and cook on low-heat for 2 minutes stirring constantly. Add chicken stock slowly to the sauce continuing to stir. Simmer over low-heat for about 1 minute or until thick. Add salt, pepper, and heavy cream. Add carrots, peas, and parsley. Mix well.

3. Cut cooked turkey into bite-sized pieces and place in pot pie mixture.

4. Butter 8 to 10 ramekin dishes. Pour pot pie filling into dishes. Top with Basic Pie Crust (p. 98). Place in oven for 25 minutes or until crust is brown. Serve with hot rice.

Basic Pie Crust

Yields 2 10-inch pie crusts

This pie crust seems to be the easiest, most consistent that I have used. This recipe always results in a flaky and tender crust that works with savory as well as sweet pies.

Ingredients

3 cups all-purpose flour
1 teaspoon kosher salt
12 tablespoons unsalted butter (1½ sticks), very cold
⅓ cup vegetable shortening (Crisco), very cold

1. 6 tablespoons ice water, plus more if dough is too thick.

2. Place flour and salt into food processor fitted with a steel blade and pulse to mix.

3. Dice butter. Add diced butter and cold shortening to machine. Pulse until butter and shortening are the size of peas.

4. Add ice water to the mixture down the feed tube with machine running. Pulse machine until dough forms a ball. Dump out on a floured board and roll into a ball. Wrap in plastic wrap. Refrigerate 30 minutes.

5. Cut dough in half. Roll one of the pieces on a well-floured board rolling from the center to the edge, turning and flouring the dough to make sure it does not stick.

6. Continue rolling for a pie. Fold the dough in half, place in pie pan. Unfold and mold to pie plate. If making pie crust to top a ramekin dish, place a ramekin dish upside down on the pie crust and cut a circle 1 inch larger than the dish. After filling the dish, place the crust on top; press the crust around edges. Slit the top and brush melted butter on sides and top of crust.

"And they gave him a piece of broiled fish, and of an honeycomb. And he took it, and did eat before them."
Luke 24:42-43

My dad, Wayne Pilgreen,

is one of the best fisherman and cooks I know. As a young boy he won several local fishing tournaments and he has been fishing at every available opportunity since. His love of fishing has connected him to the kids in a way that is unlike any other. The earliest fishing

WAYNE PILGREEN AND STRING OF BASS
Made Catch Using Worms At Pirtle's Pond

trip for any of my children was Howlett when he was just 2 days old. We went fishing at a local pond with my dad, and Howlett has loved fishing ever since.

A common bond is created because of a common interest. Dad is not just sitting on the sideline somewhere watching, he is involved in the very thing my kids love. During the spring, he takes a few of the kids at a time fishing on the lake and when the kids return home, they are full of fishing stories and are delighted that they have enjoyed a day with their granddaddy. These experiences have been most meaningful to the children and myself. In the past few years our family has had a tradition of going on a deep sea fishing trip together. Both grandfathers, their uncle Johnny, their cousin Nathan, and best friends Ryan and Zane McWhorter, take this awesome trip and catch a years worth of fish for the family. These memories are truly priceless. The men relate to one another through a common passion and experience unity as they struggle to pull

in that giant fighting Amberjack, or that huge gorgeous Snapper. There is always the fishing trip to look forward to doing during the year that creates an excitement for the future. All summer we enjoy fishing at various ponds, lakes, and the Gulf of Mexico. We are blessed that my mom, and her husband Joe, live at the lake and that we have a large creek that runs through our property in Verbena, Alabama. These are great places to canoe as well as fish.

We also stock our small pond in the winter with rainbow trout and in the summer with tilapia. I find this type of fishing a great daily diversion for the girls as well as the boys. The great thing about fishing is that just about every age, boys and girls alike, are able to enjoy the activity and it brings the family outdoors together to experience the wonders of God's creation.

Whole Bass with Tomatoes

Serves 4

This recipe is perfect for the smaller fish that need to be culled from ponds. If the head of the fish makes you squeamish, cut it off and serve the body whole. I prefer the whole fish, because I think it is absolutely gorgeous.

Ingredients

¼ cup extra virgin olive oil
1 medium onion, thinly sliced
7 tablespoons fresh mint, chopped
2 tablespoons fennel seed, chopped
2 teaspoons hot red pepper flakes
1 lb. whole tomatoes, drained
1 cup dry white wine
Salt and freshly ground black
   pepper
4 small largemouth bass, cleaned,
   gills removed, and scaled
¼ cup Italian parsley, finely
   chopped
1 cup Homemade Fish Stock (p. 47)

1. Heat olive oil in sauté pan over medium high heat. Add onions, garlic, mint, fennel seed, and red pepper flakes. Cook until onions are just brown, 8 to 10 minutes.

2. Crush tomatoes. Place the tomatoes, wine, and fish stock in pan and cook over medium heat until reduced by ⅓.

3. Place fish in large skillet or sauté pan. Pour sauce over the fish and simmer covered for 10 minutes or until fish is cooked through. Sprinkle with parsley and serve.

Fabulous Bream

Serves 4

The word *fabulous* in this title is the best adjective to describe this dish. This is truly an impressive dish to serve to family or guest.

Ingredients

1 lb. dandelions
2 cups orange juice, with pulp
3 tablespoons honey
½ cup raisins
Kosher salt and freshly ground black pepper, to taste
8 tablespoons extra virgin olive oil, plus more for drizzling
2 tablespoons balsamic vinegar
8 fillets of bream
¼ cup flat leaf parsley, finely chopped

4. In medium-sized saute pan, slowly add dandelions. Add strained orange juice, honey, and raisins. Set aside the orange juice pulp. The dandelions will shrink fairly quickly. Simmer until reduced by half. Season with salt and pepper.

5. In a small bowl add 4 tablespoons of olive oil, vinegar, ¼ teaspoon of salt, and ¼ teaspoon of pepper. Whisk until emulsified.

6. In a small saucepan, heat the orange pulp until it releases juices. Add to vinaigrette mixture. Mix well.

7. In large sauté pan heat 4 tablespoons of olive oil over high heat. Score the skin of the fillet twice. Season fish with salt and pepper. Place skin side down in pan until crispy, about 2 to 3 minutes. Flip and cook 2 minutes more.

8. Re-heat the greens. Stir in parsley. Place ¼ of dandelion mixture on plate. Put a fillet of bream on top. Drizzle vinaigrette and oil around fish. Serve immediately with French Bread with Herb Spread (p. 162).

Roasted Snapper with Mustard Sauce

Serves 4

Roasted fish does not take long at all to cook. If your freezer is well stocked with fish, this is another quick, healthy, awesome meal. Serve with a side of asparagus and this makes an incredible meal perfect to serve to guest.

Ingredients

4 red Snapper fillets
Kosher salt and freshly ground black pepper
1 cup sour cream, additive free
4 tablespoons Dijon mustard
3 teaspoons capers, drained
2 tablespoons onions, minced

1. Preheat oven to 450 degrees. Salt and pepper fish and place fillets skin side down in a casserole.

2. In a small bowl combine sour cream, mustard, onions, capers, 1 teaspoon of salt, and ½ teaspoon of pepper. Spoon over fillets covering fish completely.

3. Bake fillets for 10 to 15 minutes. Do not overbake. The fish will easily flake when it is done. Place casserole directly under broiler for about 1 minute or until the top browns a little. Serve.

Spicy Scamp with Roasted Vegetables

Serves 4

Scamp is a fish in the grouper family. It has a mild taste and is light and refreshing placed on top of roasted seasoned vegetables.

Ingredients

4 scamp filets
½ cup melted butter
1 teaspoon garlic powder
½ teaspoon salt
½ teaspoon pepper
¼ teaspoon cayenne pepper

Vegetable Ingredients

3 tablespoons olive oil
1 zucchini squash
2 yellow squash
2 tomatoes
Kosher salt and freshly ground black pepper

1. Preheat oven to 425 degrees. Slice zucchini, squash, and tomatoes into ½ inch thick slices. Place them on a baking sheet. Do not crowd the baking sheet or the vegetables will steam instead of roast. Drizzle with olive oil. Sprinkle salt and pepper over vegetables and toss well. Roast for 20 minutes or until vegetables are tender.

2. Meanwhile mix garlic powder, salt, cayenne, and pepper in small bowl.

3. Heat grill and brush fillets with melted butter. Sprinkle mixture over fillets. Place on grill for 2 to 3 minutes. Turn over and cook for 3 minutes, until done.

4. Arrange roasted vegetables on a plate. Place a piece of fish on top of the vegetables. Serve with rice or a salad with a lemon wedge on the side.

Trout in Papillote

Serves 4

This is a great dish to serve to guests in that it is simple to prepare and the fish are all done at the same time. Cooking in parchment paper is a great way to retain moisture.

Squeezing lemons are much easier if left at room temperature. Roll them on the counter using the palm of your hand to loosen the juices as well.

Very thin sticklike slices are called "julienne." They soften in a short cooking time.

Ingredients

4 trout filets
½ cup extra virgin olive oil
2 cloves garlic, crushed
Juice of 2 lemons
3 bay leaves, ground or crushed
1 teaspoon red pepper flakes
Kosher salt
1 tablespoon olive oil
1 tablespoon unsalted butter
1 sweet potato
1 Vidalia onion, sliced thinly
½ cup cherry tomatoes, halved
½ cup black olives, pitted and minced
Lemon wedge

1. Place the fish in a baking dish. Combine olive oil, garlic, lemon, bay leaves, and red pepper flakes into a small bowl. Whisk until emulsified. Pour marinade over fish and refrigerate for 2 hours, turning fish once or twice.

2. Preheat oven to 400 degrees.

3. Cut parchment paper 13 by 30 inches or large enough to hold 1 fillet of fish and ¼ of the julienned vegetables. Leave a few inches of margin to account for folding and sealing the edges. Brush each piece of parchment paper with olive oil. Remove the fish from marinade and place the fish on 1 side of each piece of the parchment paper. Season each fillet with salt. Place ¼ of the julienned vegetables and the olives on top of the fish. Enclose the fish in the paper as in photos. Brush olive oil lightly on top of packets.

4. Place the packages on baking sheets and bake for 10 to 12 minutes or until puffed.

5. Remove fish from oven and place fish on plates. Cut parchment open with a sharp knife and serve with lemons.

Using parchment paper

Cut a large 13 by 30 inch piece of parchment paper. Fold in half lengthwise. Reopen parchment paper and brush entire surface with olive oil.

Place fillet in center of ½ of the parchment paper. Arrange vegetables on top of paper.

Cover the fish with other half of parchment paper.

Begin folding at one end of parchment paper and pleat along the edges.

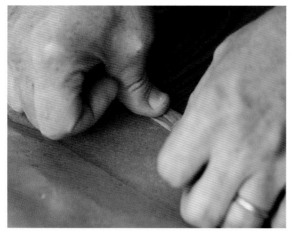

Press tightly as you pleat along the edges with a ramekin or a coffee cup.

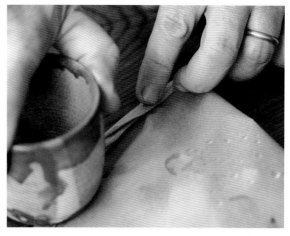

Continue pleating and pressing tightly until you encase the fillet and vegetables.

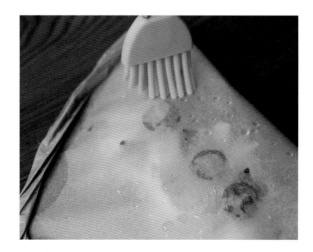

Brush olive oil across the top of packet.

Artwork by Scott Harris

Waterfowl hunting is better

than ever in the United States, therefore wild geese and duck are mainstays in many households. Wild geese and duck have a deeper, richer flavor than the farm raised varieties and are generally pretty lean. If cooked properly, cooked hot and fast or braised slowly, wild waterfowl will become a most requested dish of your family and friends.

Duck Breast with Figs and Mushrooms

Serves 4

Figs grow profusely in Alabama heat and they pair well with many ingredients, namely wild duck. This dish will surely go down as a "keeper."

Duck Ingredients
4 duck breast, boneless
Salt and pepper to taste
2 tablespoons butter
2 tablespoons olive oil

Fig Sauce Ingredients
16 fresh figs, cut in half
   lengthwise
1¾ red wine
2 cups chicken broth

Mushroom Ingredients
¼ cup butter
¼ cup onions, chopped
¼ cup scallions, sliced
   (green and white part)
1½ pounds mushrooms, thinly sliced
1 teaspoon ginger, grated
¼ cup chicken broth

Marinade Ingredients
½ cup olive oil
½ cup white wine
1 teaspoon salt
½ teaspoon pepper
1 clove garlic, crushed
1 tablespoon rosemary

Caramelized Ingredients
8 fresh figs
¼ cup honey

1. Combine olive oil, wine, salt, pepper, garlic, and rosemary in small bowl. Mix until emulsified. Place duck breast in casserole and pour marinade over duck. Marinade for 2 hours.

2. Combine 16 figs, red wine, and broth in a small saucepan. Bring to a boil then reduce to a simmer for 30 minutes stirring occasionally. Strain fig sauce.

3. Melt ¼ cup butter in sauté pan. Add onions and sauté until tender, about 5 minutes. Add mushrooms and ginger. Continue to sauté, another 3 to 4 minutes. Add ¼ cup broth and simmer until reduced by at least ½. Stir in green onions. Remove from heat and keep warm.

4. Preheat oven to 425 degrees. Place remaining 8 figs in small casserole and drizzle with honey. Bake for 10 minutes or until figs are tender and honey is caramelized.

5. In cast iron skillet, heat 2 tablespoons of butter and 2 tablespoons of oil until smoking hot. Liberally season duck with salt and pepper. Place duck in hot skillet and cook for 3 to 4 minutes or until browned and turn duck over cooking for about 3 minutes longer for medium rare. Remove to a cutting board. Let rest for 5 minutes. Slice thinly. Reheat fig sauce.

6. Divide duck among 4 plates. Place ¼ of the reheated fig sauce. Arrange 2 caramelized figs around the duck and serve.

Goose Siciliana

Serves 4

Up until the 1990s goose was a rarity in central Alabama, but during the past decade they have been plentiful. Goose is an extremely lean bird. Cooking it can be very tricky. I tried brining the goose for this recipe for tenderness, but it became much to salty. Marinating it overnight is the best option for succulent, tender meat. Pounding this meat will ensure a much more tender finished dish.

Goose Ingredients

¼ cup olive oil
¼ cup all purpose flour
Salt and freshly ground black pepper
2 geese breast
½ cup Basic Tomato Sauce (p. 155)
1 tablespoon pine nuts
2 tablespoons capers
1½ teaspoons red pepper flakes
½ cup white wine
½ cup Parmesan cheese

Marinade Ingredients

½ cup olive oil
¼ cup lemon juice
3 basil leaves, crushed
1 tablespoon brown sugar
1 tablespoon low salt soy sauce

1. In a small bowl mix olive oil, lemon juice, basil, brown sugar, and soy sauce. Marinate overnight, turning once. Remove and pat dry with a paper towel.

2. Slice goose ¾ inch thick. Pound paper thin with a meat mallet.

3. Heat oil in a cast iron skillet until smoking hot. Season the flour with salt and pepper on a medium plate. Dredge goose in seasoned flour. Add goose to skillet for 1 to 2 minutes then turn and brown the other side for 1 minute more. Transfer goose to a platter and keep warm.

4. Add the tomato sauce, pine nuts, capers, pepper flakes, and white wine to pan. Bring sauce to a boil then reduce heat and simmer for 5 minutes. Pour sauce over goose slices. Sprinkle Parmesan cheese over sauce. Serve immediately.

Wild Duck with Hash Browns and Eggs

Serves 4

This dish is simple, lovely, and versatile. You can serve this for breakfast, lunch, dinner, or any occasion. I love the way the succulent and rich egg yolk balances with the perfect duck and crispy hash browns. What's not to love?

Ingredients
2 wild duck breasts
½ cup orange juice
½ cup olive oil
1 tablespoon red pepper flakes
Kosher salt
Pepper
1 serving Old Fashioned Hash Browns (p. 146)
4 eggs
1 orange, cut into 4 wedges

1. Preheat oven to 350 degrees.

2. Place duck breast in a shallow baking dish. Combine orange juice, olive oil, and pepper flakes in a small bowl and mix well. Pour over duck breast. Marinate for at least 1 hour.

3. Remove duck from marinade. Pat dry and liberally salt and pepper duck breast.

4. Place duck breast in smoking hot cast iron skillet and sear for 20 to 30 seconds on each side. Place in oven for 3 to 5 minutes. Remove and let duck rest.

5. While the duck is resting, prepare the hash brown recipe located on page 146.

6. Divide hash browns among 4 dishes. Slice duck into ¼ inch slices.

7. In skillet in which duck was cooked, place 1 tablespoon of butter and cook sunny side up egg on medium heat. During cooking, carefully place a bowl over the egg to steam the top of the egg for 2 to 3 minutes. Place egg on top of hash browns and duck slices. Repeat with the next three eggs. Serve with an orange wedge.

Provençal Quail over Grits

Serves 4

Provençal quail is a tasty dish that leaves you wanting more. The creaminess of the grits interplays perfectly with the rustic quail smothered in rich French sauce. This is a simple, flavorful dish that could be a weekly staple.

Quail Ingredients
4 semi-boneless quails
Salt and freshly ground black pepper to taste
¼ cup butter
3 garlic cloves, minced
½ cup green onions, diced
¼ cup onions, diced
3 cups tomatoes, peeled, chopped and drained
¼ cup wine
1 teaspoon paprika

Grits Ingredients
1 cup grits
½ tablespoon kosher salt
¼ tablespoon pepper
3 tablespoons butter
5 cups water or Homemade Chicken Stock (p. 95)

1. Add grits, salt, pepper, and 3 tablespoons of butter to 5 cups of water. Bring to a boil, then lower the temperature to simmer for about 30 minutes stirring occasionally.

2. Heat ¼ cup butter in cast iron skillet until hot, but not burnt. Add semi-boneless quail (debone breast, leave leg bones in) to skillet for 3 minutes on each side or until golden brown. Remove from pan.

3. Add garlic and onions to skillet and sauté until tender. Add tomatoes and wine to skillet. Bring to a boil. Reduce to simmer until liquid is reduced by half. Add quail to pan and cook about 3 minutes or until quail is warmed through.

4. Place 1 cup of grits in a bowl or a plate and transfer quail with sauce on top of the grits or beside the grits, whichever you prefer. Serve immediately.

Grilled Quail with Caramelized Peaches

Serves 4

It is unbelievable how well sweet and tart peaches pair with quail. Scott loves this easy to prepare meal, because it is quick and simple and the grill practically does all the work for you. Invite another family to come enjoy this delightful meal from the outdoors.

Ingredients

4 semi-boneless quail
¼ cup melted butter
Salt and freshly ground black pepper
4 ripe peaches, seeded and halved
2 tablespoons dark brown sugar
1 tablespoon fresh basil leaves, finely chopped

1. Heat grill. Brush melted butter on both sides of quail. Salt and pepper the quail. When grill is smoking hot, place quail on grill for 3 minutes then turn and grill for 2 minutes more or until golden brown.

2. Sprinkle brown sugar in cavity of peaches. Add salt and pepper to taste. Place peaches on grill, skin side down, for 5 minutes. Turn peach over and caramelize brown sugar. Remove peaches from grill and top with chopped basil. Place quail and peaches on 4 plates. Serve with grits, Couscous (p. 160) or Wild Rice (p. 144).

Coq au Vin Pheasant Style

Serves 8

Wild pheasant are beautiful fowl, but can be tough if not prepared properly. Upon cooking one of our old laying hens, I thought pheasant would do well to be prepared in the same manner. I found an ancient recipe from France that I tweaked to add simplicity to the preparation and found the pheasant to be tender and most flavorful.

Ingredients

2 pheasants, quartered
3 cups full body Burgundy or red wine
1 cup Homemade Chicken Stock (p. 95),
 add more stock to cover, if needed
2 Vidalia onions, roughy chopped
2 carrots, peeled and quartered
1 bay leaf
Olive oil and unsalted butter, for browning
1 tablespoon salt
1/2 tablespoon pepper
6 slices of quality bacon, diced
1 lb. button mushrooms
2 tablespoons unsalted butter
2 tablespoons flour
Parsley
2 sprigs rosemary

1. A day in advance, clean and quarter pheasant. Place in a stockpot. Cover with wine and chicken stock. Add onions, carrots, and bay leaf. Place heavy item on pheasant to submerge them in the stock and wine.

2. The next day, remove and drain the pheasant and vegetables, keeping the wine and stock mixture for later use. Remove the pheasant to a large stockpot or Dutch oven.

3. Heat oil and butter in a skillet until smoking hot. Add pheasant for 3 to 4 minutes or until browned then turn pheasant over and brown for 3 minutes more. Transfer to stockpot. Add reserved wine and stock mixture, salt and pepper. Bring to a boil. Lower heat to simmer and cook covered for 2 hours.

4. Heat bacon and mushrooms in a skillet until brown (10 minutes).

5. Add 2 tablespoons melted butter and 2 tablespoons flour to a bowl. Ladle approximately 1 cup of the coq au vin liquid to the flour mixture. Mix well and pour into pot with the pheasant. This should thicken the sauce in the pan with the pheasant.

6. Add bacon, onions, and mushrooms in the pot, cook and stir for 2 or 3 minutes. Add parsley and rosemary when ready to serve. Taste and correct the seasonings. Serve with steamed New Potatoes (p. 140) or Perfect Mashed Potatoes (p. 150).

Countryside Pheasant

Serves 4

Wild pheasants surprises me with the intense and exciting flavor it contains. I would much prefer pheasant to chicken if properly prepared. When I cook this dish, the house is filled with enticing aromas. Serve with Rustic Bread (p. 162) and your meal is complete.

Pheasant Ingredients

2 small pheasants, quartered and rinsed
Freshly ground black pepper
4 slices pancetta
2 tablespoons butter
2 tablespoons extra virgin olive oil
3 large carrots, cut into 1-inch lengths
3 cloves garlic, thinly sliced
1 onion, diced to ¼ inch
3 bay leaves
2 sprigs rosemary
3 stalks celery
1 cup dry white wine
1 lb. whole Homemade Canned Tomatoes (p. 154),
   or 15 oz. canned tomatoes
¼ cup Italian parsley, finely chopped

Brine Ingredients

1 cup kosher salt
½ cup brown sugar
1 tablespoon peppercorns
2 scallions, chopped
2 cloves of garlic
¼ teaspoon allspice
1 quart chicken broth
2 quarts water

1. Combine kosher salt, brown sugar, peppercorns, scallions, garlic, and allspice in a saucepan. Add chicken broth and bring to a boil stirring to dissolve the salt and sugar. Remove from heat and allow to cool.

2. Combine the cooled mixture with remaining water in pot big enough to hold the birds and stir well. Add pheasants quartered and rinsed. Refrigerate overnight.

3. Remove pheasants from brine and pat dry with towels. Season with pepper.

4. Wrap each piece of quartered pheasant in a slice of pancetta and secure with a toothpick. In skillet heat olive oil and butter over high heat. Add pheasants and do not crowd or they will not brown. Transfer to plate.

5. Add carrots, garlic, onion, bay leaves, rosemary, and celery to pan and cook about 5 minutes. Add the wine and tomatoes. Crush the tomatoes as you place them in the pot. Add pheasant and reduce heat to simmer. Cook uncovered for about 25 minutes. Transfer pheasant pieces to a serving platter.

6. Adjust seasoning. Add parsley. Pour sauce over meat. Serve with Couscous (p. 160).

"For as the earth bringeth forth her bud, and as the garden causeth the things are sown in it to spring forth; so the Lord God will cause righteousness and praise to spring forth before all the nations." Isaiah 61:11

Vegetables & Sides

Heirloom Cowpeas

Rustic Roasted Vegetables

Eggplant Gratin

New Potatoes with Parsley

Wild Rice

Old Fashioned Hash Browns

Roasted Asparagus

Perfect Mashed Potatoes

Homemade Canned Tomatoes

Basic Tomato Sauce

Glazed Baby Carrots

Guacamole

Couscous

French Bread with Herb Spread

Rustic Rosemary Bread

Heirloom Cowpeas

Serves 8

Make sure bell pepper does not overcook. It will lose it's color and it's al dente texture.

Jer. 29:28 "...build ye houses, and dwell in them; and plant gardens, and eat the fruit of them."

One of my favorite memories of all time is sitting on my back porch shelling peas with my granny. She was 82 years old and still loved to spend time going and doing. She did not let much slow her down and her energy and passion for life was contagious. She canned tomatoes, shelled her own peas, and "put up" squash and okra for her famous soup and she enjoyed every minute of it. Sharing these special times with her, and the memories from participating in the vegetable preparation and preservation, has encouraged me to slow down and enjoy the simpler, more quiet, "working with your hands" work with my own children. The conversations are quite interesting and especially entertaining when talking to one another *is* entertainment. I have an idea that the memories of talking while shelling peas or shucking corn or being in the garden together are going to bring comfort and are going to be treasured by our children in years to come, as they are already by Scott and I. This is the first year we have grown these heirloom peas in our garden and they have become our favorite. They are simple to shell and simple to cook and they freeze well. We ordered the seeds from Rareseeds.com and, since they are heirloom, we will be saving the seeds, when the plant goes to seed, to plant next year.

Ingredients
4 cups heirloom fresh cowpeas
4 cups water or chicken stock for a deeper flavor
1 tablespoon salt
1 tablespoon butter
½ red bell pepper
¼ Vidalia onion
Olive oil

1. Place cowpeas, chicken stock, butter, and salt into a large saucepan. Bring to a boil. Once it reaches a boil, lower to simmer.

2. Meanwhile sauté diced red bell pepper in olive oil until al dente. Dice onion. When peas are just done (about 30 minutes on simmer) pour into bowl and sprinkle bell peppers and raw onion on top. Serve.

Rustic Roasted Vegetables

Serves 8

It is a fantastic feeling to come in with loads of vegetables you just picked, wash them off, trim and cut them, roast them, and eat them all within about 45 minutes. Sometimes we may not grow or have every one of these vegetables, therefore we just roast what we do have. Most vegetables roast very well and the flavor is best to me when cooked with this method.

Hint: use leftover vegetables in soups or stews later in the week.

Ingredients
1 Vidalia onion
1 red onion
1 small eggplant
1 yellow bell pepper, cut in thin slices
1 red bell pepper, cut in thin slices
2 tablespoons fresh basil
Salt and freshly ground black pepper

1. Preheat oven to 400 degrees.

2. Cut onions through core to keep them intact. Cut small eggplant in slices. Cut the rest of vegetables into thick strips. Place vegetables in groups on sheet pan. Do not crowd the pan or the vegetables will steam.

3. Sprinkle basil, salt, and pepper over vegetables and roast for 15 minutes. Turn each piece and roast for 5 to 10 minutes more. Sprinkle with extra salt if needed and serve.

Alice Jones runs a farm stand,

Acres Alive, in Verbena, Alabama on Highway 31 South and is assisted by her parents, Dwight and Bonnie Jones. Alice and her siblings assisted their parents in their family owned farming business, The First Great Pumpkin Patch, as well as other farming ventures. Now their children are enjoying family businesses of their own. Acres Alive is one of the most beautiful farms with the most excellent vegetables I have ever seen. Many of the very best chefs in the Birmingham area enjoy their fantastic produce.

Eggplant Gratin

Serves 4

I love to cook squash, zucchini, and tomatoes with these simple, creamy, and delightful ingredients, as well as using eggplant. Sometimes I add meat to the layers of this recipe and substitute the eggplant as noodles. It becomes a lighter version of lasagna and is fabulous!

Ingredients
Olive oil, for frying
1½ pounds eggplant, unpeeled and sliced ½ inch thick
1 cup ricotta cheese
3 large eggs
¼ cup half and half
¼ cup whipping cream
¾ cups Pecorino, freshly grated and divided
¾ cups Romano, freshly grated and divided
¼ teaspoon salt
1¼ cup Basic Tomato Sauce (p. 155)

1. Preheat oven to 425 degrees.

2. In a large frying pan, heat olive oil until almost smoking. Add slices of eggplant to pan for 3 minutes. Turn the eggplant and cook for about 2 more minutes or until browned. Place on paper towels to drain. Repeat the process until all of the eggplants are cooked.

3. Combine ricotta, eggs, half and half, whipping cream, ½ of the grated cheeses, salt, and pepper.

4. Place ¼ cup of Basic Tomato Sauce in the bottom of a medium size casserole or gratin dish. Add a layer of eggplant slices, then ⅓ cup of ricotta cheese mixture, then ½ cup tomato sauce. Repeat. Add another layer of eggplant slices then the remaining ⅓ cup of ricotta cheese mixture and top with the other ½ of the Pecorino and Romano cheeses.

5. Place the dish in the preheated oven for 10 minutes or until top is browned. Serve alone or with wild game.

New Potatoes with Parsley

Serves 8

My friend Paula gave me this recipe and I am ever thankful for receiving just about the easiest side I have ever known. We eat these flavorful potatoes at least once a week in our home. The kids can cook these with only a moments notice.

Ingredients

1 tablespoon unsalted butter
3 lbs. small white Yukon potatoes, or new potatoes, scrubbed but not peeled
2½ teaspoons kosher salt
½ teaspoon freshly ground black pepper
4 tablespoons parsley

1. Melt the butter in a large heavy-bottomed pot. Add the whole potatoes, salt, and pepper and toss well. Cover the pot and cook over low heat for 35 minutes, until the potatoes are just tender when tested with a small knife. Stir the potatoes a few times during cooking process. Turn heat off and set aside. When ready to serve add parsley.

Wild Rice

Serves 6

Our family went to our friends, Fob and Lyn's, for dinner a few years ago and they served us a fabulous meal of duck with wild rice. Lyn was so generous as to give me this great recipe. The fruit in the rice pairs really well with the duck.

Ingredients

1 cup long grain wild rice
½ teaspoon kosher salt
4 cups Homemade Chicken Stock (p. 95)
2 tablespoons butter
2 tablespoons good olive oil
2 tablespoons freshly squeezed orange juice
2 tablespoons champagne vinegar
¼ cup pecans, toasted
¼ cup dried cranberries
2 tablespoons scallions, chopped
½ teaspoon freshly ground black pepper

1. Melt butter in a medium pot. When melted, pour in rice. Brown the rice with the butter for about 3 minutes. Pour stock and salt into pot. Bring to a boil. Simmer for 1 hour. Be careful that the stock does not evaporate. If it does, add ½ cup of water to the pot. Turn burner off and cover for 10 more minutes to continue steaming rice.

2. Meanwhile, in a sauté pan cook pecans for 5 minutes tossing them often. Do not leave them in that they burn quickly.

3. Place rice in a medium size bowl. Gently incorporate olive oil, orange juice, champagne vinegar, pecans, cranberries, onions, scallions, and pepper to the rice. Serve immediately.

Old Fashioned Hash Browns

Serves 4

Hash browns make a great bed for duck, venison, steak, quail, and pheasant. The crunchy exterior and creamy interior gives the perfect texture for the rich flavors of wild game.

Ingredients
3 large Yukon gold potatoes
6 tablespoons unsalted butter
Salt
Freshly ground black pepper

1. Peel the potatoes and cut them into ½ inch cubes. Place potatoes in a large saucepan of cold water to cover. Bring to a boil. Lower to medium heat, partially covered for 5 minutes. It should be almost done. Drain and remove moisture with a towel. Set aside.

2. Melt butter in a large cast iron skillet. Once the skillet and butter are smoking hot place potatoes into skillet in a single layer. Let it brown without moving them for at least 30 seconds. Toss or turn the hash browns and leave undisturbed until browned. Continue to brown on all sides adding butter to keep potatoes from sticking.

3. Season with salt and pepper. Mash browned potatoes down with plastic spatula to caramelize the bottom of potatoes. Place a large plate on top of skillet and invert the hash browns onto the plate. Place the remaining butter in skillet and slide the potatoes back into skillet brown side up. Mash the potatoes down and caramelize on the other side. Slide hash browns onto serving platter or divide among plates and serve.

Roasted Asparagus

Serves 6

Surprisingly, all of my kids devour roasted asparagus like it is candy, especially if it is topped with shaved Parmesan cheese. This vegetable pairs extremely well with fish and quail.

Ingredients
2 lbs. fresh asparagus
2 tablespoons olive oil
1/2 teaspoon kosher salt
1/4 teaspoon freshly ground pepper

1. Preheat oven to 400 degrees.

2. If stalks of the asparagus are thick, snap asparagus at the bottom where it naturally breaks. Place asparagus on sheet pan. Drizzle olive oil over asparagus and sprinkle with salt and pepper. Roast for 10 to 15 minutes or until tender. Serve.

Perfect Mashed Potatoes

Serves 8

Mashed potatoes are a lovely accompaniment to almost any wild game dish. They are an excellent bed for meats with a sauce and they soak up the flavors perfectly. Leftovers can be used the next morning as a potato pancake by adding flour and eggs to the mixture.

When draining potatoes, remove as much water as possible or the potatoes will become gummy. Also add warm cream and butter to avoid gummy consistency.

Ingredients
4 lbs. Idaho potatoes, peeled and cut into 1-inch pieces
½ cup butter, melted
1 cup half and half, warmed
1 cup heavy cream, warmed
Salt to taste
Freshly ground black pepper

1. Place potatoes in a large Dutch oven. Cover potatoes with salted water and bring to a boil. Reduce heat to medium and cook potatoes until tender, about 15 minutes. Remove from heat. Drain potatoes. Return potatoes to pot and place back on stove.

2. Mash potatoes with potato masher. Add melted butter and half and half. Continue integrating the half and half and butter with potato masher. Add heavy cream. Mix with an electric mixer on medium speed until smooth. If potatoes are too stiff add more cream. Add salt and pepper to taste.

Tomatoes

Who can say enough about tomatoes. They are a staple in Italy and rightly so. Hunter, my oldest son, has been doing an experiment by planting many various varieties of tomatoes to see which do the best in our soil, therefore we have an abundance of wonderful tomatoes. We have had tomato sandwiches almost every day this summer. It may seem boring or wasteful to some to eat tomatoes everyday on a simple sandwich with Homemade Mayonnaise being the only other ingredient besides the bread, but I am here to say it NEVER GETS BORING EATING FRESH PLAIN TOMATO SANDWICHES. The entire family agrees with me on that important issue.

Tomatoes appeared in the United States during the 1600s from South America. People thought tomatoes were poisonous in that it favored a poisonous peach in Europe. It was also known as a poor man's food, because the rich believed they were poisonous. The more wealthy ate from pewter which contained lead and when the acid from the tomatoes combined with the lead in the plates, death would occur from lead poisoning. The poor did not have this problem because they ate on wooden plates. Well in my opinion, the rich really missed out on one of the tastiest fruits ever known to mankind.

Homemade Canned Tomatoes

To sterilize jars, boil empty Mason jars for 15 minutes or run through sterilize cycle in dishwasher. Put lids in a small pot of boiling water for several minutes. Remove. Begin canning process.

As a rule of thumb ugly tomatoes are the tastiest tomatoes. Almost all heirloom tomatoes are less attractive than their hybrid counterparts. Do not be fooled by appearances.

1. Drop tomatoes in boiling water for about 20 seconds. Remove from hot water. Remove skin from tomatoes by cutting ends off and squeezing from bottom.

2. Push down into a sterilized Mason jar. Add 2 teaspoons of lemon juice. Fasten lid tightly.

3. Submerge Mason jar in water. Bring to a boil. Once it reaches a boil continue to boil for 40 minutes for pint-sized jars and 45 minutes for quart-sized jars. Once opened, keep refrigerated. They should last in refrigerator for a couple of weeks.

Basic Tomato Sauce

Yields 1 pint

Ingredients

5 tablespoons olive oil
1 large onion, diced
1 clove garlic, finely chopped
1 lb. tomatoes, fresh or canned, peeled,
** and chopped with their juices**
2 teaspoons salt
½ teaspoon pepper
3 basil leaves, chopped

Tomato sauce is best when prepared with fresh heirloom plum tomatoes, but works well with canned tomatoes.

1. Heat the oil in medium saucepan. Add onions and cook over low to medium heat until translucent. Approximately 6 minutes.

2. Stir in garlic, tomatoes, salt, pepper, and herbs. Cook for 30 minutes.

3. With emersion blender or food processor puree tomato mixture. Adjust seasonings. Serve.

Glazed Baby Carrots

Serves 4

My little girl, Milly, would eat every one of these fabulous glazed carrots if I would give her the chance. I think she thinks they are candy on her plate.

Ingredients
1 lb. baby carrots
3 tablespoons olive oil, divided
1 tablespoon butter
½ cup brown sugar
Pinch of salt

1. Melt butter in large sauté pan. Add 1 tablespoon of olive oil. Pour carrots into pan. Drizzle the remaining oil on top of carrots.

2. Heat pan on high heat until sizzling. Reduce to medium-low heat. Add brown sugar to carrots. Mix with a wooden spoon until carrots are tender. Add a pinch of salt and serve.

Guacamole

Serves 6

This is fantastic on Venison Sliders, fish, or on the side of Venison Enchiladas. I like just eating it alone!

Ingredients
3 ripe avocados
1 jalapeno, more or less to your taste
Juice of ½ a lemon
½ onion, minced
1 medium tomato
1 teaspoon salt

Mix all ingredients in medium sized bowl. Leave it a little chunky for better texture.

Couscous

Serves 8

Couscous is small wheat pasta and is fantastic with dishes from venison to fish. Couscous is one of those dishes that is simple, fast, and delicious.

Ingredients
¼ cup butter (½ stick)
2 Vidalia onion, chopped
3 cups Homemade Chicken Stock (p. 95)
1½ teaspoons kosher salt
½ teaspoon freshly ground black pepper
2 cups couscous (12 oz.)
½ cup pine nuts, toasted
¼ cup fresh cilantro, minced
Juice of 1 lemon

1. Melt butter in a large saucepan and cook onions over medium heat for 10 minutes or until translucent. Add stock to the saucepan.

2. Bring stock to a boil. Add salt, pepper, and couscous. Put a lid on the saucepan and remove from heat. Let couscous steam for 10 to 12 minutes.

3. In a dry sauté pan cook pine nuts over low heat for 10 minutes until lightly toasted.

4. Stir pine nuts and cilantro into the couscous. Squeeze fresh lemon juice to brighten up the flavor and serve.

French Bread
with Herb Spread

Serves 8

This Herb French Bread melts in your mouth. I could eat the bread as my meal. I would not be eating a balanced diet, but it sure would be good!

Ingredients
8 large garlic cloves, chopped
¼ cup fresh parsley
2 tablespoons fresh oregano leaves
2 tablespoons fresh basil leaves
1 teaspoon rosemary
1 teaspoon kosher salt
½ teaspoon freshly ground black pepper
½ cup good olive oil
3 tablespoons unsalted butter, at room temperature
1 large loaf of French bread

1. Preheat oven to 350 degrees.

2. Cut French bread in half horizontally.

3. In a food processor fitted with a steel blade process the garlic, parsley, oregano, basil, rosemary, salt, pepper, olive oil, and butter until minced.

4. Coat the two sides of the bread with the herb mixture. Wrap the bread in aluminum foil and place on a sheet pan in the oven for 5 minutes. Unwrap the bread and bake for 5 minutes more or until warmed through. Serve hot.

Rustic Rosemary Bread

Makes 1 loaf

If you plan ahead, in that it takes the dough 18 hours to rise, this bread is easy and is worth the planning. The taste of this bread reminds me of crusty sourdough bread, but you do not have to have a starter. My kids make this bread and it goes great with almost every stew or soup.

Ingredients

3 cups all purpose flour
⅛ cup orange juice
¼ teaspoon active dry yeast
1¾ teaspoon salt
2½ teaspoons lime zest, chopped
2½ teaspoons chopped fresh rosemary
Cornmeal as needed

1. In a large bowl, combine flour, orange juice, yeast, salt, lime zest, and rosemary. Add 1½ cups of water and stir until blended, the dough will be very sticky. Cover the bowl with plastic wrap. Let dough rest 12 to 18 hours.

2. Place the dough on a lightly floured work surface. Sprinkle dough with small amount of flour and fold the dough over onto itself a few times. Cover loosely with plastic wrap and let rest for 15 minutes.

3. Coat your hands with flour and quickly shape dough into a ball. Coat a cotton towel with cornmeal. Place the dough, seam side down, on the towel and sprinkle with more cornmeal. Cover with another cotton towel and let rise until the dough is more than double in size and does not spring back when poked with a finger, about 2 hours.

4. Preheat oven to 450 degrees. Place a 2¾ quart cast iron pot in the oven until hot, 25 minutes.

5. Remove the pot from the oven. Remove the top towel. Slide your hand under the bottom towel and turn the dough over, seam side up into pot. The dough will look unusual, but that is O.K. Cover with the lid and bake for 30 minutes. Uncover and continue baking until loaf is browned, 15 to 30 minutes more. Transfer the pot to a wire rack and let cool for 10 minutes. Carefully, turn the pot on its side and gently turn the bread, it will release easily.

Desserts

Berry Parfait

Crème Brûlée

Peach Clafoutis

Dark Chocolate Flourless Cake

Easy Berry Sauce

Gray's Peaches and Cream

Blackberry Crumble

Goat's Milk Ice Cream with Honey and Brûléed Figs

Key Lime Pie Extraordinaire

Summer Fruit Crostata

Basic Whipped Cream

Stressed spelled backwards is Desserts!!!

How great is that? Sometimes around the holidays, I can get really stressed, but just knowing there awaits a dessert at the next festivity brings me great comfort and anticipation.

The children love the excitement of Christmas and we work to keep it a holiday that represents the birth of Christ, but still the busyness of the season can creep in and steal the joy that God gives freely to us. In the past few years, we have tried to simplify. It seems that as we cut back on many of the world's traditions and focus on making new traditions, those focused on Christ, my reoccurring eye twitch begins to fade.

My mother in-law, Kay, has desired that we all share desserts together to start the season before Christmas activities start piling in. This is a wonderful idea and would not be too difficult to do in that desserts are usually pretty easy, not to mention yummy.

I am trying to enjoy every holiday and moment that I have with my children while they are still at home. I am learning not to let busyness steal my time and much needed energy from my family. I love watching and listening to the kids talk to each other about what they are going to make or purchase for another sister or brother. They truly love to bless their siblings. It is rarely, if ever, quiet in our home and especially around Christmas, but I would not have it any other way. I want to soak it up while I can, and I hope to always remember the laughter and joy of family chatter that filled the rooms of my home during the celebrations of Christ's birth.

Berry Parfait

Serves 4

This is not only an extraordinary healthy dessert, it is gorgeous. Serving this at the most elegant events would get rave reviews. This is an awesome breakfast dish as well and the granola can be used as a cereal on its own.

Ingredients
1 cup old fashioned oatmeal
½ sweetened, shredded coconut
¼ cup almonds, sliced
¼ cups pecans, chopped
3 tablespoons melted butter
2 tablespoons honey
10 strawberries, sliced
½ cup blueberries
2 cups honey flavored Greek yogurt

1. Preheat oven to 350 degrees. In a large bowl mix oatmeal, coconut, almonds, and pecans with the butter until well incorporated. Pour onto a sheet pan and bake for 10 minutes.

2. Remove pan and turn mixture. Place granola back into oven and bake for 10 more minutes, or until golden brown. Loosen granola from the pan with a wooden spoon. Set aside and let cool.

3. Slice strawberries. Divide ⅛ of the strawberries and blueberries among 4 tall glasses. Divide ⅛ of the yogurt among the glasses. Divide ⅛ of the granola among the glasses. Repeat with another layer of fruit, yogurt, and ending with granola. Drizzle honey over the granola and serve.

Crème Brûlée

Serves 6

I think this has to be the top dessert in the world! It is always a perfect ending to a perfect meal. My daughter, Graylyn, surprised our family with this creamy dessert and without fail she is begged at least weekly to serve it after dinner.

Ingredients
1 quart heavy cream
1 vanilla bean, split and scraped
1 cup sugar, divided
6 large egg yolks
2 quarts hot water

1. Preheat oven to 325 degrees.

2. Place the cream and vanilla in a medium saucepan set over medium-high heat and bring to a boil. Remove from the heat. Set aside for 15 minutes. In a medium glass bowl, whisk together the egg yolks and ½ cup sugar until it starts to lighten in color. Add cream in a drizzle stirring continually. Pour the mixture into 6 8-inch ramekins. Place the ramekins into a large casserole or roasting pan. Heat enough water to come ½ way up the sides of the ramekins.

3. Bake 35 to 40 minutes or until the crème brûlée is set but the center is still jiggly. Remove the ramekins from the casserole and cool to room temperature. Refrigerate for at least 12 hours and up to 3 days.

4. Remove the crème brûlée from the refrigerator for at least 10 minutes prior to browning the sugar on top. Divide the remaining ½ cup sugar equally among the 6 dishes and spread evenly on top. Melt the sugar with a torch or broil on high in the oven to form a crispy top until browned. Allow the crème brûlée to sit for at least 5 minutes before serving.

Peach Clafoutis

Serves 8

Clafoutis is a simple peasant dessert that is absolutely delicious. Almost any fruit can be placed in a baking dish with the batter simply poured over it and baked for a fast, tasty end to a great meal. We usually make 2 and save one for breakfast.

Ingredients
½ cup of milk
1 tablespoon unsalted butter at room temperature
1 cup heavy cream
⅓ cup plus 2 tablespoons granulated sugar
2 teaspoons pure vanilla extract
6 tablespoons all purpose flour
3 large eggs, at room temperature
1 teaspoon grated lemon zest (2 lemons)
¼ teaspoon kosher salt
2 to 3 peaches, firm but ripe
Confectioners' sugar

You can use frozen berries, thawed and drained for the fruit in the recipe.

1. Preheat oven to 375 degrees. Butter a Pyrex pie plate or a casserole about 1½ inches deep. Sprinkle 2 tablespoons of sugar on the sides.

2. Pour into blender or food processor the heavy cream, sugar, eggs, vanilla extract, flour, lemon zest and salt. Cover and blend on medium for 1 minute. Set aside for 10 minutes.

3. Meanwhile, peel, quarter, pit, and slice the peaches. Fan the peaches out in the pie dish or arrange peaches in a casserole. Pour the batter over the peaches and bake for 45 to 50 minutes in preheated oven or until top is brown and custard is firm. As the clafoutis cools it will sink down a bit. Serve warm or at room temperature with confectioners' sugar sprinkled on top.

Dark Chocolate Flourless Cake

Serves 10

I love flourless desserts! I am a true chocolate lover and the great thing about it is that dark chocolate (in moderation) is quite healthy. Not only does dark chocolate contain antioxidants which keeps the body from aging by blocking free radicals, it lowers blood pressure and balances hormones in the body. Who could believe something that tastes so great could be so good for you! This dessert is a little time consuming to prepare, but it is SO worth it!

Ingredients
2 cups of butter (2 sticks), cut into ½ inch pieces plus extra for greasing the pan
1 lb. good bittersweet chocolate (Callebaut, Ghirardelli, or Hershey), coarsely chopped
3 tablespoons of strong coffee
9 large eggs, cold
Confectioners' sugar, for dusting

1. Preheat oven to 325 degrees.

2. Place parchment paper on bottom of 9-inch spring form pan. Grease sides of pans with butter. Wrap outside, bottom, and sides of pan with heavy duty foil. Place pan in roasting pan.

3. Melt butter and chocolate in a Pyrex bowl over a saucepan filled with 2 inches of simmering water. When barely melted, stir in coffee and remove from heat.

4. Place eggs in mixer and mix on high speed for 3 minutes or until eggs are pale yellow. Continue whipping 3 more minutes or until eggs have doubled in size, approximately 4 cups.

5. Fold ¼ of eggs into chocolate mixture with a rubber spatula. Do not over mix. When incorporated add ½ of remaining mixture and when that is incorporated add the last ½ of eggs. Place batter into spring form pan and smooth.

6. Heat 1 quart of water in microwave or in a saucepan to a low boil and pour around the spring form pan until the water reaches half way up the sides of the pan. Place pan carefully into the oven. Bake for 20 minutes or until cake has risen slightly or thermometer inserted registers at 140 degrees. The cake will not look done. It will firm up in the refrigerator. Remove cake from water bath and let cool at room temperature. Do not remove from pan.

7. After cake has cooled, wrap in plastic wrap. Cover top with foil and refrigerate overnight or for 8 hours. Unwrap cake and remove spring form pan. Sprinkle with confectioners' sugar. Serve with fresh berries or Easy Berry Sauce (p. 178) and Basic Whipped Cream (p. 192).

Easy Berry Sauce

Yields 1 pint

I like to use frozen berry mix when I am in a hurry or the berries are not in season. Do not add water to the saucepan. Place the berries into the saucepan. Add the sugar. Bring berries to a simmer. Add vanilla and a few more berries to add texture.

Ingredients

3 cups fresh blackberries, raspberries, strawberries, or a mixture
¼ to ½ cup sugar, depending on your taste
1 teaspoon vanilla extract

Bring 2½ cups of berries, ¼ cup of water and sugar to a simmer over medium heat. Cook for 2 minutes or until sugar is dissolved and berries are cooked through. Add the remaining ½ cup of berries to mixture and incorporate. Serve over chocolate cake or ice cream.

Gray's Peaches and Cream

Serves 4

When I was a little girl (a long time ago) my grandmother would chip up peaches, put them in a bowl, and pour in milk and sugar for us to eat together right in her kitchen with the door open in view of the fig tree and laundry line in the back yard. This is another blessed memory in my mind for which I give much thanks to God.

I prefer raw local honey.

Ingredients

4 peaches
4 cups milk
1 cup cream
¼ cup mild honey
1 vanilla bean

1. Peel and pit peaches. Cut peaches in wedges and place in bowl.
2. Combine milk, cream, honey, and vanilla. Stir mixture briskly. Pour over peaches just to cover. Enjoy!

"My son, eat thou honey, because it is good; and the honeycomb, which is sweet to thy taste." Proverbs 24:13

Blackberry Crumble

Serves 10

In the spring our family loves to go pick wild blackberries and come straight home to make this wonderful blackberry crumble. Everyone takes their own zip top bag and competes to get the biggest and the most berries. It reminds me of the doors opening on Black Friday, the day after Thanksgiving, when all of the bargain hunters go shopping for Christmas.

Topping Ingredients

1 cup all purpose flour
⅓ cup granulated sugar
⅓ cup brown sugar
1 teaspoon cinnamon
⅛ teaspoon salt
½ cup pecans, chopped
1 stick butter, room temperature

Filling Ingredients

5 cups blackberries
1 tablespoon granulated sugar
3 cups brown sugar
5 tablespoons flour
1 teaspoon vanilla

1. Combine flour, sugar, cinnamon, salt, pecans, and butter in a bowl of an electric mixer fitted with a paddle attachment. Mix on low speed until the butter is the size of peas. Set aside.

2. In a large bowl combine blackberries, sugar, flour, and vanilla. Pour blackberry mixture into a casserole.

3. Crumble the topping mixture evenly over the blackberries. Bake for 45 to 50 minutes or until the tops are browned and crisp and the juices are bubbly. Serve warm with Goat's Milk Ice Cream (p. 184) or Basic Whipped Cream (p. 192).

Goat's Milk Ice Cream with Honey and Brûléed Figs

1 gallon

Goat milk has many health benefits. It is high in calcium, phosphorus, potassium, iron, copper, magnesium, and antioxidant activity. People who are lactose intolerant often revert to goat's milk and have no problems thereafter with digestive issues.

Ice cream made from goat's milk has an exciting flavor paired with honey and figs. There is really nothing that compares to its fresh, mild flavor.

Ingredients

4 fresh eggs
2 cups sugar, plus 2 tablespoons
½ vanilla bean or 3 teaspoons vanilla extract
½ teaspoon kosher salt
1 pint half and half (you can use goat's cream instead)
2 quarts fresh goat's milk
8 figs
2 tablespoons of honey, for drizzling

1. In a large bowl, whisk together eggs, 2 cups of the sugar, vanilla, salt, half and half, and goat's milk. Pour mixture into a ½ gallon ice cream maker and freeze for about 20 minutes.

2. A few minutes before serving ice cream, half figs and place them flesh side up on a baking sheet. Add remaining ¼ tablespoon of sugar on top of each fig. With a torch, brûlée the sugar on top of the figs.

3. Scoop ice cream into small bowls on serving dishes and top with 2 brûléed figs. Drizzle honey on top of each serving. Serve immediately.

We have friends, Gene and Suzy Bloom,

that introduced us to beekeeping. They come over every Friday morning at 7:00 a.m. and help us with the hives. We are loving learning about bee behavior and LOVING the honey.

Key Lime Pie Extraordinaire

Serves 10

Key lime pie is a staple food for Southerners. The tart taste of this pie with no flour nutty crust is sublime (no pun intended). You will never go back to the graham cracker crust once you have tasted this combination.

Pie Ingredients
3 cups sweetened condensed milk
½ cup sour cream
¾ cup key lime juice
1 tablespoon grated lime zest

Flourless Crust Ingredients
½ cup hazelnuts, toasted and finely chopped
½ cup pecans, toasted and finely chopped
2 tablespoons honey
1 tablespoon butter, melted
1½ teaspoons cinnamon
Pinch of nutmeg
Pinch of salt

1. Preheat oven to 350 degrees.

2. Combine chopped nuts, cinnamon, nutmeg, and salt in a small bowl.

3. Whisk melted butter and honey in another small bowl.

4. Add nut mixture to the butter. Mix well. Press mixture into pie plate and bake for 10 minutes in preheated oven.

5. Meanwhile, combine condensed milk, sour cream, lime juice, and lime zest to a medium bowl. Mix well and pour over prepared crust and place in preheated oven for 5 to 8 minutes, or until small bubbles surface on pie. It may not look done, but remove from oven and allow to cool. Cover and place in refrigerator for at least 6 hours. Serve with Basic Whipped Cream (p. 192) and top with a slice of lime.

To skin hazelnuts toast nuts for 5 to 10 minutes (watching closely so that nuts do not burn). During this time the nut will swell. The brittle skin will not stretch and will crack. Remove from oven and set aside for at least 20 minutes. Rub nuts together in hands to remove skin.

To aid in juicing the key limes, heat in microwave for 1 minute.

Summer Fruit Crostata

Serves 6

This is another simple recipe that is used as breakfast as well as desserts in our home. The only problem is the oldest four kids want a whole tart for themselves.

Ingredients

2 pears
½ cup blueberries
¼ cup all purpose flour, plus 1 tablespoon
¼ cup granulated sugar
¼ teaspoon salt
2 tablespoons unsalted butter
1 egg white beaten
1 Basic Pie Crust (p. 98) or premade Pillsbury
   pie crust
2 tablespoons raw sugar

1. Preheat oven to 350 degrees. Roll pie crust into an 11-inch circle on a lightly floured surface. Transfer to a sheet pan.

2. For the filling, cut pears in wedges and place them in a bowl. Toss them with the flour, sugar and salt. Fan the pears on the dough circle leaving a 1½-inch border. Sprinkle blueberries on top of pears. Fold over in sections. Use egg wash as glue as you work in sections around the dough. Spread remaining egg wash over folded dough. Dot the Crostata filling with butter.

3. Sprinkle raw sugar over entire tart and place in preheated oven for 20 to 25 minutes or until golden brown. Serve with Basic Whipped Cream (p. 192).

Basic Whipped Cream

1 pint

For the very best whipped cream make sure bowl, whisk, and cream are very cold.

Ingredients

1 cup heavy cream
3 tablespoons confectioners' sugar
1 teaspoon vanilla extract

In a large bowl, whip cream until stiff peaks are just about to form. Beat in sugar and vanilla until peaks form. Do not over beat or it will turn to sweet butter.

"As arrows are in the hand of a mighty man; so are children of the youth.

Happy is the man that hath his quiver full of them..." Psalms 127:4-5

Recipe Index